Asperger's Looking In From The Outside

By Sally Watson

Copyright © 2015 Sally Watson

All rights reserved.

ISBN-13: 978-1511863759

The names of people in this book have been changed, but the experiences described are real events.

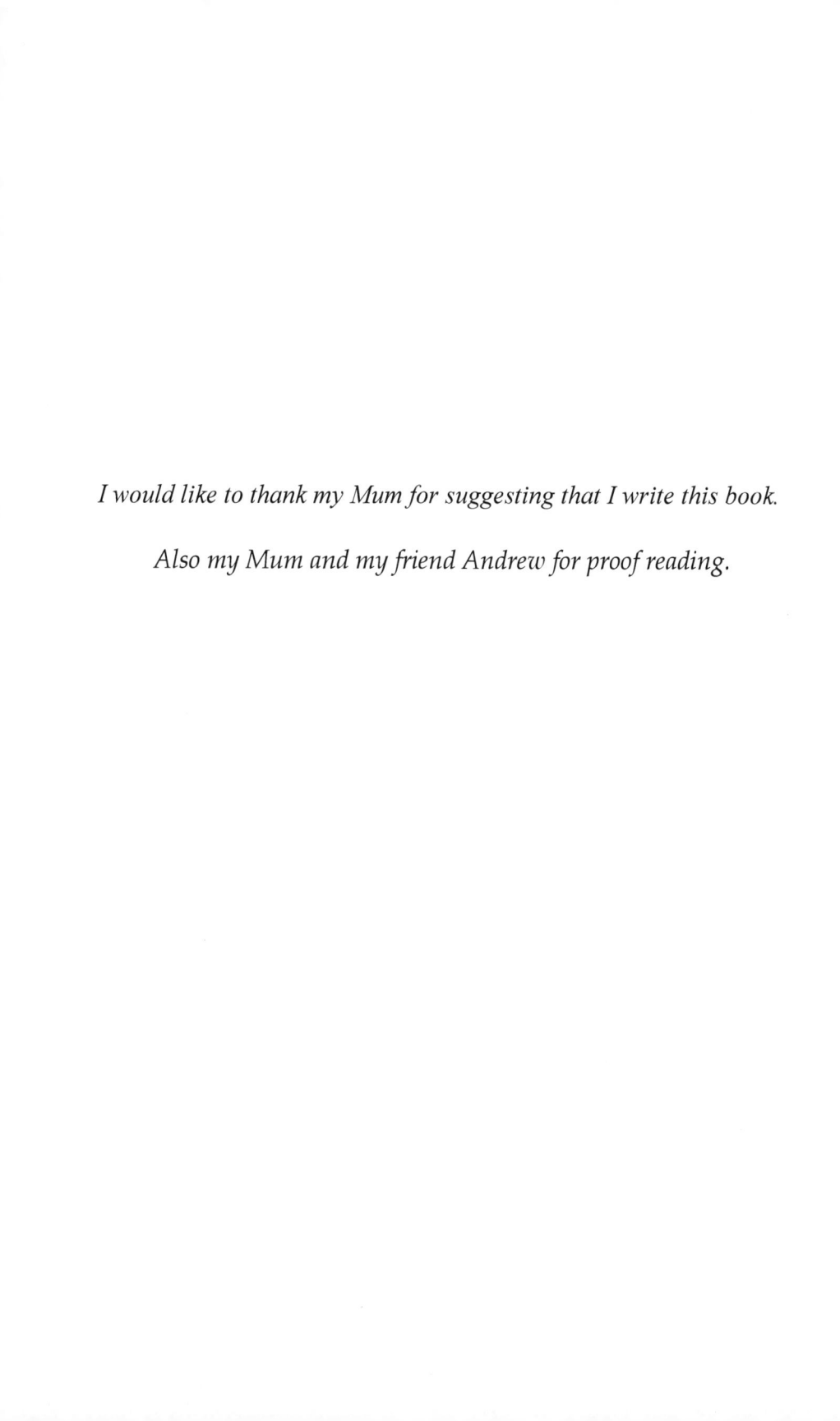

I would like to thank my Mum for suggesting that I write this book.

Also my Mum and my friend Andrew for proof reading.

Chapters

Chapter 1, Living With Asperger's   1

Chapter 2, My First School   5

Chapter 3, My Next School   10

Chapter 4, Mainstream School   12

Chapter 5, My Last Year in School   16

Chapter 6, Holidays   18

Chapter 7, My Gran   20

Chapter 8, Poppy   25

Chapter 9, My Dad, The Stranger   27

Chapter 10, College First Year   31

Chapter 11, College Second Year   35

Chapter 12, Job Centre and Work Experience   39

Chapter 13, College Again   46

Chapter 14, Counselling Service   51

Chapter 15, Seeing the Doctor   54

Chapter 16, Office Work Experience   56

Chapter 17, Yet Some More Work Experience	58
Chapter 18, Job Opportunity	60
Chapter 19, The Diagnosis	63
Chapter 20, What Happened Next	67
Chapter 21, Five Months Work Experience	69
Chapter 22, Paid Work	71
Chapter 23, Temping Job	82
Chapter 24, Last Temping job and The Job Centre	88
Chapter 25, My Two Visits to See the DEA, at the Job Centre	91
Chapter 26, Change of Benefit	94
Chapter 27, Moving House One	97
Chapter 28, Moving House Two	101
Chapter 29, The New Home	105
Chapter 30, Miss Paint	108
Chapter 31, Church	113
Chapter 32, Driving Lessons	116
Chapter 33, My First Homegroup in the Church	123
Chapter 34, My First Car	127

Chapter 35, Homegroup Two   130

Chapter 36, Art Group   133

Chapter 37, My First Art Exhibition   136

Chapter 38, Andrew   139

Chapter 39, Atos   142

Chapter 40, The Job Centre for Three and a Half Months. 144

Chapter 41, Andy's Help with Benefits   149

Chapter 42, Asperger's Support Group   152

Chapter 43, The Table Sale   155

Chapter 44, My Dad Not the Stanger Anymore   158

Chapter 45, My Hobbies and Other Things That I Enjoy   161

Chapter 46, Final Conclusions and Thoughts   166

Chapter 1

Living With Asperger's

I'm not sure how I am going to start this book, about my life. It is my Mum's idea that I write a book, sharing the story of my life.

I'm hoping that by writing this book, other people who are living with Asperger's, will realise, that they are not the only ones with it. Before I went to a support group, for people with Asperger's, I felt that I was the only one, in the whole wide world with it. My Mum and Dad have tried to understand me, but it's not the same, as being with other people, with similar problems, as yourself. You don't feel so alone, as there are other people with, Asperger's out there.

I was born with Asperger's, a lifelong condition. It affects me in my communication with other people. I find it hard to start a 1conversation with people I don't know. Some of the time, I wait until someone comes and talks to me. You can be left standing or sitting on your own, if you are waiting for someone to come and join you. Everyone else knows how to join groups of people, who are already in conversation. I don't. I don't want to be in the way. Plus I have no idea of what to say. What do people talk about, when you don't know them? My mind just goes a complete blank. If you are standing there saying nothing, some people think that you are not interested in what they are saying and they move onto talking to someone else. I'm all right if I know people well and I like them. It can be very lonely when you have to go to gatherings of people, and you are there, with no-one even noticing that you are there. Twice I have left, as soon as I was able. No-one wants to stay anywhere, when they are invisible and don't feel wanted. It makes you feel worthless and not as good as others. Also it reminds me that I will never be one of them, however hard I try. I will always be an outsider, trying to pretend, that I'm one of them.

I don't like to tell people that I have Asperger's. I get worried about how they might react towards me. There has been so much bad press, about a few people with Asperger's. Some think we are all computers hackers or that we are going to lose our tempers and make some sort of scene. The newspapers don't write anything good, about Asperger's in their paper, good news, doesn't sell, bad news does. I wish there was some good news about people like me. It makes us all seem as though we will do something that we shouldn't. It's just not true. I like computers, but I wouldn't try to break into anyone's system.

In all walks of society you have different personalities. Some personalities are more prone to breaking the law than others. If you are poor, it doesn't mean that you are more likely to steal than if you have pots of money. Rich people steal as well as poor. Of course you will have some with Asperger's, who will break the law, but not all.

It does worry me a lot about what people will think of me. I don't want to be classed as this strange person, you have to keep an eye on, in case I do something that I shouldn't. People can sometimes think you are slow. In my opinion, if you don't say much, people can think you are unfriendly, or boring, or stupid or uninterested, in what they are saying, which in my case isn't true. I just want to be normal, which I am not going to get. I was born with Asperger's and there is no cure, if there was, I would be first in line. As I just want it to go away, so I can join in everyday life, like everyone else is allowed to do, instead of watching others, buy houses, have jobs, get married, and generally get on with their lives.

Not being able to fit in some of the time, makes you feel worthless and in the way and that you have nothing to give to the world. Even people with Asperger's should be able to give their skills and talents to the world. In the end it erodes away your confidence.

Well I had better start this book. A good friend of mine said, that I should start at the beginning. So I will start with my earliest memories.

Chapter 2

My First School

I was born two weeks late, on the 18th November 1975, late afternoon. I was supposed to be born, on the 4th November.

My Mum said that she got in trouble when she went into labour. The nurses told her off for making too much noise, they told her that she would frighten the young mums. I was a really big baby, I weighed 9lbs and needed my nails cut straight away, after I was born, as they were so long.

I don't really remember much, until I stared school, at the age of four.

The only thing that I remember is getting sand in my mouth, at playgroup. The playgroup was very close to where we lived, just five minutes away. I remember not liking having the sand in my month.

Years later when I told my Mum the story about the sand in my month, she recalled that "one day she went and picked me up from playgroup and that I was crying and that they couldn't find out why, as I wasn't able to tell them, what it was that had upset me, as I couldn't speak." Perhaps it was the day, I had got sand in my month.

I had all sorts of tests, to try and find out why I wasn't talking. All they came up with was that I was a bit slow. I understood everything what was being said to me, I just couldn't respond to anyone. So when I was four, I was sent to a special school for children with learning and behavioural difficulties. It was a small school, about ten to fifteen in each class.

The children came from all over the county. So in the holiday times, you didn't see any of your friends. I didn't mind not seeing other children in the holidays. I was used to finding things to do on my own.

We had a smallish garden in which I used to spend a lot of time in looking at the insects. I used to collect them up and put some in jars and try sometimes to bring them into the house. Mum didn't like insects in the house. She thought that they might escape from the jars and run all over the place.

The first day I went to school I didn't want to go. Mum said that I cried when she put me in the taxi. Mum said the next day I couldn't wait to go. Personally I can't remember, my first day.

Some boy during my fist year got into trouble. He had kicked some other child. The teacher got this poor boy to stand in the middle of the classroom and got us all to stand around him and kick him, so that he would know what it was like to be kicked. I just stood there and watched from the outside of the circle everyone else kicking this boy. I just felt that what the teacher had asked us to do was wrong. I didn't like watching what was happening in front of me. I know this four or five year old boy shouldn't have kicked this other child. The teacher should have punished the boy in some other way.

The Headmaster left a term or two after I started at the school. At the time he seemed really, really old!!! He looked like one of the oldest people on the planet. In reality he was probably only sixty or sixty five. But at five years old anyone over thirty is really old. My parents seemed ancient when I was little!

I watched the Headmaster from a distance walking once, he swung his legs up in the air, bending them at the knee. I suppose he thought it was funny. There were several children around him, following him across the playground as he walked in this strange manner.

My sense of humor back then wasn't all that good. So it just looked strange, the way the Headmaster was swinging his legs. It just didn't make any sense. What was the point of it?

The last year, in my first school, was the best one of all. I got on well with the teacher and the classroom assistant. I had nicknames for them both. One I called 'Curly Wig' and the other 'Curly Top'. They both had curly hair. Neither of them minded being called that. These days you wouldn't be allowed to call the teachers by any nicknames, you might think up.

I also got on quite well with the headmaster. It was in the days, when the headmaster came out of his office, onto the playground and actually talked and played with the children. I remember running around with the other children, playing with the headmaster. Headmasters don't have time, to get to know the children in their schools these days. It's all paperwork and meetings.

All of my friends in the early days of school were boys. I was quite a tom boy.

The last year I was at my first school, I made friends with a girl called Sally. Sally didn't go with me to my next school. She went onto main stream, I think in a small village near where she lived. I didn't see her ever again. I wonder what she is doing now. Quite often in class, I would borrow her pencil sharpener. She always liked you to blow into the sharpener, after you had used it. She didn't like any little bits left in it. Sally was very particular about how she liked to keep her pencil sharpener. It's what I most remember about her.

I was upset and shocked, when I found out, that I would have to move onto another school. It never came into my mind, that one day, I would have to leave and go to another school. Even though there wasn't another year, after the last one I was in. It never occurred to me that I would have to move onto another school.

I remember sitting up in my small box bedroom at home crying about it. There was no talk about having to move onto another school, at the end of that year.

Chapter 3

My Next School

When I started my next school, it seemed so big. There were about eighty five children, over seven years, junior and senior. For each year there was just one class, no different streams for different abilities. The idea was that, as the classes were small you would be able to work at your own pace. Up until my last three years there, it seemed to work.

I never liked the school. It wasn't so friendly or nice, as my first school.

On my first day another pupil got hold of my coat hood and pulled it really hard. I had to grab hold of my coat, from around my throat, to stop it from strangling me. None of the dinner ladies, who were standing out in the playground, that day, did anything about this girl, hurting my throat. I don't suppose they would have done anything, until I dropped unconscious, on the playground. Not a very good start, to a new school.

I went up early into the next year. I can't remember how early. There was another girl in my class, for some reason or other, she was a year behind what she was supposed to be, so we went up together, into the next year.

So I was over a year in the next year. Just as well I liked the teacher, a Mrs Wales, she was my favorite teacher, of my second school.

The first thing she seemed to say was, 'last year I had someone, who told me where I had left my red pen, as I am always leaving it somewhere in the classroom.' So I thought that, I will tell her where her pen is whenever she leaves it somewhere in the class.

Mrs Wales, was much friendlier than the teacher I had in my first year at my new school. The teacher in the first year complained one day when I kept getting the letter 'A' wrong, in the alphabet that I was trying to learn to say out loud. I wasn't trying to get it wrong all the time, but the way she carried on, you would have thought that I was. In the end she smacked the top of my leg. I don't think that is anyway to teach, to frighten your pupils into getting it right.

A few years later, I got on better with the teacher I had in my first year, she seemed a bit friendlier towards me.

Chapter 4

Mainstream School

By the time I was 11 years old, another girl and myself were asked if we would like to go to mainstream part-time. We both answered, "yes", if the other went as well. I was the one who went, but without my friend.

The school was so big, so many classrooms. I don't know how many.

At first I went just for English. I was assigned a classroom assistant for all of my lessons. I would wait in the reception area for my classroom assistant and we would then go to my lesson.

I was rubbish at English. There was a lot of things that I didn't know. Everyone else had learnt what I did not know, early on in their school years. So I was way behind them. I don't know why they sent me for English, the school must have known, that I would be a long way behind, everyone in the mainstream school. I was second from the top in my other school. The girl who was asked about coming with me, in my opinion was the top for English. I don't know why she didn't come with me, perhaps her parents said no, to her coming.

One day I was waiting for my classroom assistant to arrive. I waited ages for her to come, in the end I went across the reception area, to the main desk and asked them where she was. They didn't know, so I had to go to the class without her. I was worried what I was going to tell the teacher, as I was now quite late for class.

On the way I had to go up some stairs and I must have been turning my feet over in a funny way. As these two girls called me spastic. I didn't say anything to them.

When I got in the classroom and said why I was late, she didn't tell me off, which I was concerned about. Perhaps she knew that my classroom assistant wasn't coming.

I never saw my classroom assistant again. No one told me that I was losing my classroom assistant. One day she was there, the next she was gone.

They started to send me to math's next, then science. No one asked me how I felt about it, or how I was coping with the school. No one cared about me.

The following year was worse than the first. I arrived for the science lesson. New classroom, new teacher and only one person who I knew. I said to this pupil 'where is everyone we know.' Her replay was 'they are in different classes.' No one had bothered to tell me that each year, everyone moves to different classes with different teachers. That is what happens in mainstream. It came as a shock, as I had no contact with anyone from mainstream.

The science class the second year was a nightmare, no one wanted to learn anything. They would throw chairs about. Talk when the teacher was talking. Not much learning got done. The previous year was so different, the teacher managed to engage everyone's interest in what he wanted to teach.

The whole class was kept back one lunch time. I was supposed to be going back to my other school. The teacher never said you better go Sarah. In the end I had to say to her, that I was supposed to be at my other school. There was no problem she let me leave. I was worried that the teacher wouldn't let me leave her classroom, to the next lesson and I would get into trouble for not going back.

I did make one friend, who was also from a special needs school. I met her in the science class in the second year. We were friends for about four years.

Things came to ahead in the third year of being in the mainstream school.

When I was thirteen I started to get a lot of migraines. Every now and again, I would have time off school. All I could do was lie in bed, groaning. The migraine usually lasted about 5 hours. Mum didn't know what was causing them until about three years ago. She thought it was just me going through puberty. I think it was all the stress of the main-steam school. Not understanding the unwritten social rules. It was like an alien planet, but without the guide book, or someone to show you around.

Anyway going back to things coming to ahead. Mum said that I came home one day from the mainstream school and cried. I don't remember crying. She couldn't find out why. I remember Mum taking me to see the Doctor and having to wait outside, while Mum talked to the Doctor on her own. I don't know what was said. Soon afterwards, I was pulled out of the mainstream school. My parents thought it was that I couldn't cope with the work. I had no idea what the school thought. They probably didn't care. They never asked me how I was getting on.

I think my experience in the mainstream school is still effecting me today. I just didn't get the help I needed, to be able to integrate into the classroom.

Chapter 5

My Last Year in School

The teacher I had in my last year at school, wasn't very pleased with my parents for pulling me out of the mainstream school. She told them so when my parents went for the parents evening, to see supposedly, how I was getting on. Not that I had learned anything that year, or the previous two years. The last three years of school were a complete waste of my time. I would have learnt more from sitting all day every day, just watching the TV. All that happened in the last year was that I came home every day completely tired. I was so bored, repeating what I already knew.

The teacher was good at two things, the first was, finding everyone the work placement that they wanted. The second was keeping the discipline, in the class, as the teachers that I had the previous two years, were useless at that.

I was so glad when I could leave. As my birthday fell in the November, I was allowed to leave at Easter.

I went around the school, the last half an hour, saying goodbye to each teacher. Each teacher, I said goodbye to, I thought I'm so glad that I don't have to see you again. What a relief to get away from the place! When the bell went, I ran as fast as I could, out of the school. Hooray! I don't have to come here, five boring days of each week. No more wasting my time in school, hooray, hooray and hooray!!!!

My school years still affect me today. I don't feel as good as everyone else. Everyone else in the world, is so much better than me. It has left me feeling at times worthless. At times I also feel that I'm in the way.

Chapter 6

Holidays

Every year while I was growing up we would take a week's holiday. Just the three of us, Dad, Mum and me. My Gran's sister Iris, would come down for a week, from the Midlands and stay with my Gran. If she hadn't come down for a week, we wouldn't have been able to go away for our week's holiday, Gran would have probably had to come with us. Or we wouldn't have gone away at all. As Dad would not have wanted to leave his Mum, on her own for one week.

Each year we went to Sanford Park cavern site, in Dorset which is near Poole, and stayed in a static caravan for the week. I had a week off school, which then was allowed. We used to try and go at the end of September, when it was cheaper.

I really looked forward to this week away. It was always over too quickly and then it would be back to going to school and everyday things. As a family we never did much together. But this one week in the year, we would be spending time together and doing things as a family. Not just going to places that my Gran wanted to go to.

The caravan site in the end was like a second home, as we went throughout my childhood and into my teens. We went nowhere else, as Mum and Dad couldn't afford to go on holiday more than once a year. If we needed to go home to my Gran, it was only about five hours away, so we would have been able to get home quickly. Luckily we never needed to cut short our holiday.

Chapter 7

My Gran

I have no brothers or sisters. Nor do my parents. We are all only children. So I have no Aunties or Uncles. Up to the age of seventeen and a half I had a Gran. She lived in the same house as us downstairs with her dog Poppy. My Gran had her own lounge, kitchen, bedroom and loo. We lived up-stairs. Our rooms were, two bedrooms, lounge, kitchen, bathroom and loo. My Gran lost her husband after only 12 years of marriage. He died of cancer. My Dad at the time was 11.

My Mum also lost her Mum, when she was 16 of TB.

It wasn't always easy living in the same house as my Gran. When I was young I didn't really see that it was a problem for my Mum. It was nice to be able to go downstairs and see my Gran, whenever I wanted to. We used to play a lot of board games. Snakes and Ladders, was one we used to play a lot. Gran and I also liked spinning knives and those spinning tops. Anything that would spin, really. Gran also liked to draw cats, with big human like teeth. Mum still comments on those cats now. Even though it's over twenty years since she died. It has stuck in Mum's mind for some reason. I don't know why.

It was a problem whenever we went out, as we all had to go and say goodbye, to my Gran, before we went anywhere. We couldn't just go. When we all came back, we had to go and see my Gran again. It wasn't just a quick goodbye or hello, we're back. You would be there, at least five minutes or so. My Mum got fed up with having to see my Gran, whenever we went out and came back. Looking back on it, it just wasn't normal to have to see my Gran to say goodbye and hello we're back. At the time, it didn't really bother me, as it seemed perfectly normal thing to do. We always did it. If we had not seen my Gran, it would have been strange to me.

To me it seemed normal, seeing my Gran every day. For my Mum it was a big life change when she married my Dad. She had been living on her own, until she was 39 years old. She knew if she didn't agree to go and live in the same house as my Gran, that Dad would not have married her. Mum gave up a lot of her freedom, when she got married. My Gran never liked my Mum. Whoever Dad married, Gran wouldn't have liked or got on with. She was frightened that my Dad would go away, and leave her all on her own. Just like her family did after the funeral, of her husband in 1952, none of them offered to help my Gran, she was completely on her own bringing my Dad up. So she went to South Africa to live for about nine months. She had a brother out there. Unfortunately they fell out and my Gran and Dad came back to England. My Gran had bad health most of her life. She went into the bed and breakfast business, after she came back from living in Africa. She wanted my Dad to marry, but not to leave her. She thought it wasn't healthy for my Dad to be single.

The last few years of Gran's life, we didn't get on so well. My Gran didn't seem to like me so much. I think she thought I was too much like my Mum, whom she never really took to. I spent less and less time with my Gran, towards the end of her life.

My Mum was always kind to my Gran. The last years of her life my Mum nursed her. She cooked all her meals. Cleaned all her rooms. Did everything for her. My Gran had lots of mini strokes, which meant that she lost her speech, mobility also became very difficult. She couldn't move from one room to the next, without any help. She also had trouble breathing. It must have annoyed her that she had no choice, but to accept my Mum's help, as my Dad was at work all day. I was at school, then college. So my Mum was left to clean the house cook all the meals, nurse my Gran, go food shopping, ironing everything in the house that needed doing.

When my Dad came back from work she had to listen to all my Dad's problems arising from his working day.

When you marry you leave your Mother, at least that is what is supposed to happen and partly it did. But my Dad's work came first, then my Gran, Mum 3rd and then there would be a big gap and Dad would sometimes notice me, but never when I did something good, only when I was naughty.

My Gran took ill, while Mum and I were away on a short holiday. My Mum needed a few days break from looking after my Gran full time. We had gone away on a coach holiday to Hull, for five days. We had just finished going around Lincoln Cathedral and were sitting on the coach, when someone came from inside the Cathedral asking if my Mum was on the coach, as they had her husband on the phone. My Mum came back and said that my Gran had been taken into hospital.

The coach driver was very kind to my Mum. He made all the arrangements for us to go back home that night, by taxi. We were due to go home the next day. The coach driver felt really sorry for Mum, after she told her story, about what it was like at home. I think that he felt Mum was some sort of saint, to put up with my Gran and Dad. On the way home, we only stopped once or twice, just for the loo.

I remember my Dad saying that my Gran said, "thank you for all you have done for me", as she was going into the ambulance.

That was the last words she said to my Dad before she went into a comma. I think she knew she was going to die and it was her last chance to say thank you. My Gran never said "thank you", for anything. It was so unlike her, so I think that she knew that she was going to die and it would be her last chance to say 'thank you'.

My Dad was in pieces over his Mother dying. He was just way too close to his Mother, it just wasn't healthy.

Then within a few months where my Dad worked, they were privatizing the department my Dad was in and they were looking to get rid of some of the older workforce. So my Dad opted to go. If he had waited another year, he probably would not have got the same offer. He didn't really want to retire. His work was everything to him. It gave him status in life. He felt somebody at work.

So he lost his Mother and job in a very short span of time. The two things that were most important in his life. Dad probably would have missed Mum and me less if one of us had died. Me the least.

So for all of us, it was not a very good time in our lives.

Chapter 8

Poppy

Poppy was my Gran's dog, she was a Jack-Russell. A Jack Russell can be snappy, Poppy never was. Poppy was born two years before me. Luckily she was never jealous of me. Dogs can be jealous of babies, but Poppy liked me more than I liked her. I have just never really taken to dogs.

My Dad used to take Poppy every day for a walk, first thing in the morning before he went to work. There was a small park near where we lived, about five minute's walk away. Even at weekends he would take Poppy over to the park. My Dad was more attached to the dog than my Gran ever was. Poppy was more like a family dog, even though she lived down stairs with my Gran. My Gran feed Poppy and paid all of the vet bills.

Poppy died at 19 years of age. Towards the end of her life, she couldn't hear well, or see that well as she had cataracts. She would get confused when she went outside to do her business, she would just stand there and look at a plant, not realising why she was out there. Poppy also would have little accidents indoors. In the end my Gran had to have her put down, as she was getting thinner and thinner.

Dad was very upset when my Gran had to make the decision to have Poppy put to sleep. Dad felt like he was losing a member of the family. Mum and Dad took Poppy to the vet. Dad waited outside in the car, while Mum went in with Poppy. Mum felt really guilty when she went in, as Poppy was looking up at my Mum, in a really trusting way. Mum stayed with Poppy, while the vet put her to sleep.

Afterwards Dad had Poppy cremated. For about twelve years, Poppy's ashes were in the wardrobe, in my parents' bedroom. When they went to sleep at night and when they awoke the next morning, Poppy's ashes were there. It wasn't until we moved, that Poppy's ashes left their bedroom. I suppose they must be somewhere in the roof of our new place.

Chapter 9

My Dad, The Stranger

My Dad didn't really bother to get to know me, until I was twenty five years old. He was so taken up with his Mother and his work. Which meant that there wasn't much time for Mum and I.

When I was born he was interested. He wasn't there at the birth, as men waited outside in those days. My dad got to see me before Mum did. Poor Mum who had carried me around for nine and a half months, had to ask to see me. "Can I see her", said my Mum. Dad and Gran went home and drank all the sherry, which was supposed to be kept for Christmas, while my Mum was stuck in the hospital with me.

Nearly all of my upbringing was left to my Mum. Dad seemed to only notice me when I was doing something wrong.

All my Dad was interested in was his Mother and his work. His Mother was no 1, in his life. She always came first, me last.

My Dad used to work a lot from home. He wasn't very good at sharing an office with other people. The other people in the office, would always make too much noise and irritate him.

When Dad was working from home, Mum and I, would have to be really, really quiet. We would have to creep past the bedroom, where he was working. No noise was allowed. Even normal walking wasn't acceptable when passing the bedroom. You had to be like you were in someone's house, in the middle of the night and you were stealing their things. If you made any sound, you would get yelled at. Mum was much better at being quiet, than me.

Dad would work in the evenings and also the weekends. He thought that he was indispensable. He thought that his place of work, would fall apart without him.

So while I was growing up, I didn't really see a lot of my Dad. He just worked, worked, worked and worked. That's what I really remember most about my Dad, while I was growing up. He just worked. He was a workaholic, though he wouldn't have agreed with that.

He would keep saying to my Mum "I just have no choice, I have to do this." Mum accepted his behavior. She also accepted, his absence, as a husband. She knew she was way down the pecking order. I wouldn't have accepted it. I would have got a divorce.

At meal times in the evening before he went to work in the bedroom, Mum and I would have to listen to him going on and on and on, about the people he worked with and all they had done to annoy or upset him during the day. It was so boring sitting there having to listen to it night after night. Meal time took so long, listening to all my Dad's moaning. I wasn't allowed to leave the table, until Dad had finished eating. Dad took at least forty five minutes each night. Those forty five minutes, were the most boring part of each day. Even more boring than school and that was saying something.

When he wasn't working, Dad would spend a large part of any spare time, with his Mother.

Dad never realised, how he treated me when I was a child, was wrong. It has probably led partly to my feelings of worthlessness and feeling that everyone else is better than me. He has never said that he was sorry. He just thinks that he has made up for it since. Dad has spent a lot more time with me in the last few years. But it never makes up for all those years, when I was a child growing up, that he missed out on. He seems to think that it does. Dad thinks that I should forget, that he didn't spend much time, with me and just move on from there. But I can't, it hurts that he was more interested in his work and mother than his only child. After all, it was more my Dad, that wanted a child, than my Mum. Once he got me he didn't want me.

Chapter 10

College First Year

I went to college in September 1992. The people in my class, at school, did go before the summer holidays, for one month, to get us used to going to college. None of us from my school got a choice of what course we went on. I didn't realise until I had got sometime into the year, that I was allowed to pick my own course. Also what some of the other courses were? It might sound a bit odd. But no one said to me there was a choice. I didn't know anyone who had been to college. So it was all new to me. My Dad had been to college, first on a course one evening a week, when he left school, then again in his forties, for one day a week and one evening a week, both times to do with the work, he was paid to do. But things were different back then. Plus Dad when I was sixteen, was more interested in his work, than my future. I only went to college, as England then was in a recession and I hoped that in two or three year's time, it would be over and I might stand a chance, of getting some paid work.

I hated the course that was picked for me. It was just like being at school. I didn't learn anything. Some of the people in the class mucked around and were quite often late. It meant that you couldn't get on with the class. You would start the class, then you would have to recap, on the first twenty minutes, for instance when someone came in late. Not only were the classes boring, but I had to put up with people, I didn't like, in them as well.

I did make two new friends. Jan and Andy. Andy was a 'case', he would bring to college everyday his haversack, with just his pen inside. It made Jan and I laugh, Andy carrying around this haversack with just his pen in it. Andy was tall about six foot. Neither Jan nor myself saw him outside college. I did keep in contact with Andy for some years after we all left college. Jan is still in contact with Andy.

We all did meet up once after we left college. Andy came from Exeter to us to see us both. Jan and I enjoyed the day. Hopefully Andy did as well.

I was friends with Jan for about three to five years. It didn't really end all that well. I won't go into what happened.

We did become friends again for about eighteen months. But it was hard to meet up, as Jan was quite busy. When she wasn't busy, I was doing something. We did phone each other up, but after a while it stopped.

Jan sometimes comes to the same church as me, so I do get to catch up with her, when I'm able to.

Going back to college, there was this one class that really got on my nerves. It was once a week. One of the lessons we had to write down how we would make a cup of tea. I've known how to make a cup of tea, since I was about ten, probably younger than that. What a complete waste of time.

Another lesson was about how to wash a floor. You must make sure that you don't walk on the bit, you have just washed. Start the far end of the room and make your way towards the door. I know that. Its common sense, I don't need to be told that.

The lessons were so tiring and dead boring. Once a week for three hours. They went on for the whole year. There was five of us in the class. I was so glad when the classes came to an end.

During the year we all worked towards getting a certificate for Youth Award Scheme, in either bronze, silver, or gold. It was never clear what course work went towards this certificate. The tutors never thought to tell us and I didn't think to ask them. I was just so bored the whole year.

When the end of the year came, Jan got silver, which I think she deserved as she had worked really hard. I got a bronze. One of the other ones, who came in late and hardly did any work, also sometimes just didn't turn up, for class, got a silver. Which I didn't think was right. The only different work he did to me was, that he did sport once a week, while I was in that class learning how to make a cup of tea. I worked all year and came in on time. I only disappeared once to the town, when I was supposed to be in class. So I didn't think the certificate was worth the paper it was written on. It was so unfair. Perhaps if I had caused lots of trouble I would have got a silver. The only one thing that I learnt all year was, that bad behavior is rewarded and good behavior isn't.

When the whole course came to an end, I was pleased as I didn't like most of the other people on the course. I thought next year can't get any worse. I was so wrong. Now I never say that things can't get any worse, as they can.

Chapter 11

College Second Year

My second year, I went on the General Education Course. I wanted to go on this course the first year, after I heard about it, but I wasn't allowed. One or two from my school who were in their second year at college, were allowed on the course.

The main subjects were Math's, English and IT (information and technology), by the end of the year you got three qualification in these subjects. I managed to get foundation in Math's, City and Guilds in English level one and IT.

The actual course was what I thought it would be. But the other people on the course drove me around the bend. Some of them just didn't want to work, they would turn up late, then muck around, which made it hard to teach the few of us that wanted to learn. There didn't seem to be anything the tutor could do to improve their behavior.

One class I was in, it was so bad. I sat at one end of the room, the short end. The two long ends were down the side from me. There was this young man, who must have been about sixteen, or seventeen, who clearly had some sort of problem. The trouble makers sat on the other long side, tormenting him, while the class was going on. In the end he lost his temper and chucked his table right across the room at them. The teacher never tried to stop them picking on him. I didn't see this young man again. I don't know what happened to him. I felt sorry for him.

One of the trouble makers had got expelled from two schools and had to go to college by law, so he just didn't want to be there. Why did he have to end up in my class? He shouldn't had been in anyone's class. He had forfeited his chance twice before, why give him a third chance.

For a short while there were two other ladies in the class. One left, I don't know why. Nicola went on another course with her friends. Her gran was dying of cancer. She couldn't cope with them calling her names, as well as her Nan dying. It was unusual for Nicola to get picked on. At school she was the most popular girl in the class, everyone liked her. No-one ever called her names.

In the end I just went for the lessons, which involved getting my qualifications. The rest of the time I was part time on another course. Which also was a waste of time.

The IT part of the course was all right, as I was in the end the only one which turned up for it. There were supposed to be eleven of us. The teacher didn't stay in the class for most of the lesson. He would just go somewhere else, then come back to check up on me, then vanishes again. It was the best lesson of the week. I could get on with the lesson, without any trouble from the other people in my class. I've never been in a class like it, where the teacher wasn't there for most of the lesson.

Going back to the trouble makers in my year, things came to ahead towards the end of the year. I think there were only a few weeks to go before we finished the course. We still had all our exams to take. I was coming back from lunch. One of the other people on the course, saw me and said, 'don't go in the classroom, there has been a fight.'

So I waited around the corner for the tutor to come along. I didn't want to get caught up in any trouble. When I saw him I told him what I had been told and we entered the classroom together.

What a mess. Chairs and tables all over the place. Also a hole in the door. The tutor had to go and see someone about his classroom. When he did come back, the three trouble makers had been expelled. One of the people who had been involved in the fight, was that boy who was 15. One of them, had put his foot, part of the way through the door. There had been four people involved. The 4th one who hadn't been in any trouble, during the year, just managed not to get expelled, with the tutors help. He put in a good word for him. He had been one of the two, in the fight.

After that the last few weeks were, nice and quiet. The tutor was allowed to get on with teaching.

I was supposed to be going back to college for a third year, but after all my trouble the past two years, I couldn't be bothered. Plus the course I thought I would do, I decide wasn't quite right for me. As I would have to go and interview managers about their work and I was too nevus to go and do that. I wasn't able to say boo to a goose. I didn't think about doing another course instead. Perhaps if the two years I had done already, I had enjoyed, I would have tried to look for another course. But I somehow don't think it would have occurred to me, thinking about going on another course. I just didn't think like that back then.

Chapter 12

Job Centre and Work Experience

After I left college at eighteen, Mum took me to the job center to sign on. I was about three months off my ninetieth birthday. After about two months, I got to see the Disability Employment Advisor (DEA).

I only got to see the first one once, as she died on my ninetieth birthday. I didn't think we were going to get on though, but I was sorry that she died, of a heart attack. She wasn't all that old. In her 50's, I would say.

The next DEA, when I was nineteen sent me on work experience, cleaning in an old people's home. Which went well, as I got on all right with the other cleaners and the laundry lady. The care workers were a bit odd. They would sometimes compline about bits of the cleaning they thought I had missed. Which I hadn't, as some of the residences, would go into their rooms and make a mess after you had just been there and cleaned. And they would drop something in the hallway, not meaning to.

I have done work experience in three care homes and only one, I didn't find that the care workers, were funnier.

There was no job at the end of the ten week work experience.

Next I got sent to another old peoples' home. Washing up this time, which I didn't ask for, I asked for cleaning. I hate washing up. Eight to one o'clock five days a week. I was so bored! When I went home I was tired, from being bored. I didn't get on with the care workers, they were an odd lot. They seemed to look down on me, they thought I should be doing more than just washing up in my five hours. But there wasn't time. At breakfast time each residence had, one tea cup and saucer, one teaspoon, knife, plate, teapot, toast rack, bowl and spoon and two other pots. Times that by 20-25 people, it keeps you busy.

Then it would be coffee time. I went to get the trays ready with the drinks on them. Then you would wash them all up.

After I had my own coffee, I would have to lay the tables up for dinner.

Twelve o'clock, it would be time for dinner. More washing up.

Towards the end of the ten weeks, I realised that there would be a job for me there. I couldn't stand the thought of having to work there, for the next forty years. I thought that I would be trapped and not be able to ever get away and work anywhere else. The thought of working there horrified me, I just couldn't stand the thought of it. I managed to leave before my ten weeks were up.

I wasn't very popular with the DEA at the job centre or my dad, they both thought I was lazy.

It was just so depressing washing up, with no escape, until I was sixty five. I didn't think I would be able to leave. People wouldn't think, you were able to do anything, apart from washing up. I already felt worthless, this washing up job, just made me feel worse still.

My next work experience was as a care worker for two weeks. I only stayed one week.

When I met the lady who owned and ran the care home, there was something I didn't like about her. If you have asked me what it was, I couldn't have told you. The lady from the benefits, who went with me to the interview, said afterwards she was nice, wasn't she. I went along with her and agreed.

She was supposed to pay my bus fares and give me £1.50 a day for a meal. I never saw a penny. So I was right not to like her. She claimed she didn't understand how it all worked. So I lost out. Mum paid my bus fares, so that I wasn't out of pocked. Otherwise it would have come out of my, benefit money.

Another thing, she asked me to stay a little longer one day, which I agreed to. I asked to use her phone, so I could ring Mum, to let her know, that I would be later than I said I would be. It was a phone where you put money into it. The residents I presume used it. She gave me some money to put in the phone. The way she gave me this money, you would have thought she was doing me a huge favor, instead of me doing her a favor. It was only about 20p. It was not like she was paying me any money for being there. I just got my benefit money and nothing else.

There was a job there. The pay was terrible £2.50 an hour for the first six months, then £3.50 an hour after that. The hours would have been twelve hours for five days, then six hours on the sixth day. Which she thought was a half day. One full day off each week. Holidays were one week paid and one week unpaid. The lady who ran the home wouldn't be able to get away now, with paying this little to her care workers, or giving only two weeks holiday with only one week as paid time off. It must have been around 1998, when I was twenty one.

I couldn't have worked there, I didn't like seeing the old people naked or taking them to the loo. You have to be someone really special, to work in an old people's home, I think. Not everyone can do that sort of work. I don't feel very comfortable, getting so up close and personal with people. I'm not someone who likes to hug people. Some people these day like to hug you each time that they see you. I hate it! I say that I rather not hug. People must think that I'm a little bit odd. So seeing old people naked isn't for me. I wouldn't be able to touch them. I would soon had got the sack.

The next idea the DEA came up with was a course in finance as I said I would be interested in having a job in an office. So Dad and I went for the day to Leatherhead where there was this sort of college with all different courses to do with getting people back into work. They had a good success rate, with finding people jobs at the end of their courses.

There were other people there on the open day. We were all shown round. The bedrooms were so small, you couldn't have walked one pace across the room from your bed to the wall. The wardrobe was so small, it was about half the size of a normal one. The wardrobe was right at the end of the bed. There was no gap between the bed and wardrobe. The room was very drab, a sort of brown beige colour, a rather depressing brown beige colour.

The whole living quarters seemed to be in this brown drab beige colour. The whole place looked like it was in the 50's still.

We were told that there was one bathroom to eight people. Which worried me, as I take quite a long time. What if someone was in it, I would be late? What if I held up the other seven people? I thought I just can't cope, with eight people, sharing one bathroom.

The more I saw and heard, the more it sounded like a prison. It would be too far to go home each weekend, which meant I would have to stay there most weekends.

They did have a bus that they used at the weekends, to take the students down to the town, if you wanted to go. In the evenings there were activities you could go to. Which I wouldn't have gone to, as I would want some time to myself.

So I would be sitting in my bedroom, which you couldn't swing a cat in, seven evening each week. It would be like sitting in your cell. It would have been the better of the two evils. I don't know what I would have done. I suppose I would have sat on my bed and read. There was no room for a chair in the room, or TV. There wasn't any room to put your suitcase anywhere. The wardrobe went from the floor to the celling, so you couldn't have put it on top. I suppose it would have gone in the wardrobe. Less space then, for your clothes.

The people on my course, seemed to be into fishing and talked about going fishing each weekend. It didn't appeal to me. Even If I didn't fish, I would have to talk to them. I just want some peace and quiet, when I wasn't sitting in the classroom. I'm not used to being around people all the time. At home, I spend most of my time, on my own.

I decided it wasn't for me. I was glad when it was time to go home.

The DEA wasn't very pleased. She complained that I had turned down those other two jobs and now I was turning down this course. I wasn't able to articulate then how I felt about the course. She just thought I was lazy. The other two jobs just were not suitable for me. At the time, I asked for cleaning, not washing up or working in a care home. I just wasn't able to articulate to her, how I felt about anything.

Chapter 13

College Again

When I was twenty three, I went back to college and spent a year studying for a foundation businesses GNVQ.

The course itself was good. But the behaviour of the other students wasn't all that good. They would sit in the classroom and play games on their computer, when they were supposed to be doing their work. Not that it distracted me too much, as the computers didn't have any sound. The computers would sometimes blimp. It seemed to come from the computer tower.

Most of the students had just left school. A few were older, about three that I can remember.

I didn't make any friends as I didn't fit into the class. I wasn't into computer games and mucking around playing computer games in class. My only reason for being there, was to get my GNVQ, not to play games, on the college computers.

I did talk to the others a little, but I had nothing in common with any of them. So at lunch times, I spent all of my lunch times, on my own.

I got on well with the tutor, who ran the course, she would explain what she was teaching well and she didn't mind if you asked her again, which I would sometimes.

We also had a trainee teacher, which I just couldn't get on with. She was a right pain. At the end of her lessons I would save my work, but the computer I would be on took ages to save my work, which annoyed her. She said that I should start saving my work sooner, as I was holding up the next class, coming in. She didn't complain to the ones who were playing games in her class. She seemed to take a dislike to me.

Her lessons were hard to understand, she took us for information technology. She would give us a sheet of paper with instructions on what to do on the computer, which I found hard to follow. Her instructions were so long winded. If she had used all the short cuts on the computer, her instructions would have taken up half the paper. Then I wasn't used to the computer, so half the time was taken up with reading and trying to understand what she was getting at, which wasn't easy. Everyone else in the class, had been using a computer for some time, but I was new to it. I had gone on a short course, before starting my GNVQ, to learn how to use Microsoft Word.

Another tutor would sometimes come in and observe her teaching us and I suppose mark her on her performance.

The last lesson she came in and told us her tutor had failed her, which didn't surprise me, as I thought she was rubbish at teaching and had an attitude problem. But she told us she had gone above him and got her fail mark overturned. She had some nasty things to say about her tutor, which I didn't think was appropriate. You don't tell a whole class what you think of your tutor. No one else seemed to think it was inappropriate as they all liked her, it was just me who couldn't get on with her.

At the end of the year three of us finished on time. I and two others managed to obtain a merit. The rest were given extra time to finished their work. Which I didn't think was right, as they should have been working, during the year, instead of playing computer games. If they had been studying and working they would have finished on time. The rest the tutor said, got a pass mark.

As I was on the New Deal, I had a bus pass, which I could use on the bus, to get my Bus fares half price. One day I got on the bus, after college and asked for a ticket, like you do. The bus driver for at least half the journey, had a go at me. He said that the bus pass, was only meant for you going to work and home, not for attending college. I tried to tell him, that it was also for going to college, but he wouldn't have any of it. Everyone on the bus must have heard him having a go at me, for using my bus pass. What's it to him, you would have thought it was coming out of his own wages. The driver just wouldn't give me a ticket, that's why I stood there, for about half the journey. I wasn't happy about the way the bus driver treated me. My mum was also not very happy, so she had a word with her cousin, who works in the bus company about the bus driver. It was so embarrassing standing there, with the whole bus, watching what was being said. Also there were two or three students, from my class, who were travelling on the bus. My mum's cousin managed to track down the driver, but I don't know what happened to the driver. As far as I was concerned, the bus driver got away, with treating me how he liked.

The tutor was bit worried, as I hadn't made any friends and thought it would be a good idea, to go and see the college counsellor. So I agreed to go and see the college counsellor.

I stood nervously, outside the counsellor's office waiting. When he arrived, I was surprised because I assumed it would be a lady. I wasn't expecting a man, for some reason, I thought the counsellor would be a woman, which made me a bit more nervous. He sort of slinked past me and unlocked the door.

I went three times. But we didn't get anywhere, as I didn't know why I was there. There wasn't anything wrong with him, I just didn't know why I was there. How was he supposed to help me, if I didn't know why I was seeing him?

All we ended up talking about was how I would carry out a relationship if I had a boyfriend. I said 'that I would live with the man for a while, to see if we would get on living together, before I would marry him.' You don't want to marry someone and then find out, you don't like living with them. They might drive you around the bend. The man might do something that really annoys you. It's better to find out, beforehand than afterwards.

The councillor said that his children, lived with their partners for two years, before they were married. Just to see if they got on living together.

After the course I went on a short course for three weeks, to improve my computer skills and at the end of the course, if you passed you got a certificate. Which I managed to pass. I can't remember what the certificate was.

I had an interesting conversation with the tutor who was running the course, about the trainee teacher in my GNVQ, which I had some trouble with. I found out that the other tutors, also had problems with her. No one seemed to be able to get on with her. If I had known this, while I was on my course, I may have complained, about how she treated me.

Chapter 14

Counselling Service

Just before we went to Open Door, Mum read this article in the paper about a man who was in his sixties, who had a lot of trouble fitting into life. Some of what this man was like sounded like me. He was married. He had just been diagnosed with having Asperger's Syndrome, which I had never heard of before. I said to Mum 'that sounds just like me', Mum agreed with me.

So not long after reading this piece in the paper, Mum took me to see a counsellor. I don't know if this counselling service is still running now, but back then, it was for adults between 18-25 years old.

We waited twenty to thirty minutes, past our appointment time. In the end, mum went and spoke to them. They had forgotten all about us sitting waiting. I was already nervous, all the waiting just made it worst still.

This lady counsellor came soon after. Mum wasn't allowed to go upstairs with me. It was their policy to see the clients, without their parents being present. The clients were supposed to be able to open up more, when their parents were not in the same room. It had the opposite effect on me. I just found it hard to explain why I was there. When I told her that Mum and I thought, that I might have Asperger's, she seemed to understand. She asked me then, 'if I would prefer to have Mum with me.' I said 'yes.'

So she went and got mum. Mum told the counsellor why we had come to see her. She listened and decided that it would be better, if I went and saw the Doctor first. As the help she might give me, might not be right. We agreed with her.

On the way out, I went to the loo. I had never been in a loo like it. There was a basket in there, with lots of condoms all in different colours. It unsettled me a bit. I was already feeling a bit panicky, after all that waiting, then having to see the counsellor, for a while on my own. I suppose some of the clients had sexual issues. The loo was an eye opener. Hopefully I will never see a loo like it again.

I never been so glad to get out of somewhere before. Not that there was anything wrong with the counsellor. She was friendly, to Mum and I. It was just that the atmosphere, made me feel anyhow. I was out of my comfort zone.

Chapter 15

Seeing the Doctor

So soon after going to open door, Mum took me to the appointment, with my Doctor. Mum explained to the Doctor about this article in the paper. Mum told the Doctor about all the social difficulties, which I had all of my childhood and then into my adult life. I just didn't understand, how to fit in, with the rest of the world, when in a social situation. I could never think of what to say and people wouldn't talk to me. They would just take no notice of me. It was like, I wasn't there, which was not nice. I didn't like going anywhere, where you would have to make small talk. I would just sit there and say nothing.

The Doctor had never heard of Asperger's, so she had to go and talk to one of the other Doctors. When she came back in, she agreed to write a letter to try and get me seen by someone, who could diagnose me.

For instance, I hated seeing my Dad's cousins once a year. We would have a meal, which seemed to take forever to eat. They would all talk. I would just sit there, or go to the loo. I could get some quiet in there. One year while having this torturous annual meal, I got a headache. So I went and sat in the loo. It was the only way I could cope, hiding in the loo. No one else would be in the cubical with you.

Chapter 16

Office Work Experience

After my course I went back with my Dad to see the DEA at the job centre. We discussed me doing some work experience in an office.

So I went to the social services offices for three weeks. The two people that I worked with, I got on really well with.

There was a bit of a funny lady in the office up from ours, which no one could seem to get on with. She was the union representative for the offices. I was told that she kept tabs on all the comings and goings of everyone. She knew what time you came in and what time you left. It made her really unpopular.

One day I needed to use her computer, as the two in our office were in use, so I went and tried to use hers, as she wasn't there that day. But I couldn't get in, as she had pass code protected it.

The other two whom I was sharing an office with, thought that it was typical of her, to do something like that.

For the three weeks I worked with a lady and a man, fairly close to my age, a little older than me.

The man used to share an office with her, but in the end he changed offices, as she was so difficult to be in the same room with. She complained that he sat too close to her. Which he denied. I never had any trouble with him, nor did anyone else, that I know of.

At the end of my time there, the two people that I was working with, bought me a dictionary and gave me a voucher, to say thank you for all my work, which was a nice gesture.

Chapter 17

Yet Some More Work Experience

The next course of action was that the DEA sent me on some more work experience, at the local Town Hall for five weeks. It was supposed to last for six weeks, but they took on someone new, while I was there, so there wasn't any space, for me to be able to do my last week there. I got on fairly well with the other people, who I was sharing an office with, until the new person started. Then I seemed to be in the way. They didn't seem to know what to do with me. It was a shame, as up to this point, we all seemed to get on well. We all joked with each other. But it was all a new ball game, after the new person started.

The DEA wasn't very pleased when I didn't get a job there. She seemed to think that I should have got a job there. It was all news to me that she thought that I should had been taken on as an employee. To me I was just there, to gain some work experience in an office. I think that she thought, I should have got the job that was going there. I don't think that I was up to the job that this other lady got. It all upset the DEA. I seemed to get the blame for them not taking me on. I didn't think that it was my fault. I was never told about this job until I was well into my work experience. Even then I didn't know what all of the job entailed. Only a small part of it, which I didn't think I could do.

Chapter 18

Job Opportunity

At this time, I had a job opportunity, at the job centre, where there was a good DEA working.

Somehow she knew about this charity that I think was based in London. I don't know much about them. But they knew about this man, who had a disability and needed someone, to type his work up for him on the computer.

So this man from London came down to meet me. He wasn't much to look at. He had holes in his jeans. He took no care what so ever in his appearance. It rather surprised me, that someone would come to work, looking such a mess. I didn't think it was on. When you go to work you should look smart. Of course if your job is messy, than you don't wear smart clothes. But he was meeting people in their own homes. I liked him though, as a person. It just shocked me, what clothes he came to work in.

So I went with a support worker from the job centre, to see the man who wanted help with his admin. We saw him in his own flat. We all sat in his lounge and discussed what the job would be. The man was at least twenty years older than me. We all seemed happy about it. He said "yes", that he would have me. The job was for twenty hours per week. The pay was good either £7, £8 or £9 pounds per hour. The job seemed ideal for me, as I wanted to do some data imputing. This was when I was twenty four years old.

So we all went away, happy with everything that was talked about.

I had an appointment with the DEA, at the job centre, a few days later. My Dad went with me. She was not happy. For once, it wasn't anything I had done wrong. It was this disabled man, who had upset her. He had changed his mind, about wanting me to do his computer work, for him. I don't know what had changed his mind. But the DEA, was flaming mad about it. She said, "I want to punch his lights out."

So that was the end of the job. I was disappointed and upset about not getting the job, as it seemed ideal for me. But if he was like that, perhaps it was a good thing I hadn't started to work for him, as he might have changed his mind, after I stopped signing on at the job centre.

At least this DEA, wasn't blaming me for it all going wrong. She wasn't at our job centre for long. She moved to another one, in a town about forty five minutes away. It was a shame as I seemed to be getting on all right with this one. All of the other ones I had trouble with. They all found fault with me. I was always in the wrong. It was never the DEA's fault. It was never that she had found the wrong type of work, or a course that was too far from home and an unsuitable atmosphere that I would go more into my shell than I was already in.

Chapter 19

The Diagnosis

Eighteen months passed before I received an appointment with a clinical psychologist. I had two appointments, which lasted one hour and thirty minutes each.

One of the tests the psychologist did, was adding up some coloured straws. She said to me, I have nine red straws and five yellow straws and two blue straws, how many straws do I have? I was trying to keep all the different straws apart and how many there were. I don't know if I gave the right answer. Really the question was what is $9+5+2=$, it wasn't about the straws at all. I think that I asked her to repeat it several times. If the math's question had been written down, it would have been easy, to take it in and remember, what I was being asked. I have always had trouble with math's questions that are long winded. I normally have to read them more than once, to understand what

I'm being asked. I'm thinking what is it they are really asking? I know that they are just trying to make the math's, a bit more interesting, but I would rather just get down to the bones, of the question.

While I was having my test, I had to listen to this tape, of someone talking and say how I thought they sounded. What emotional state, I thought they were in.

One of the other tests was putting coloured plastic blocks into a pattern. You had to copy a picture. The psychologist had this picture at an angle which didn't suit me, as I wanted it straight. So I kept on straightening the picture, but the psychologist kept putting it back to an angle. I tried to move my head to an angle so I could try and see what I was supposed to be doing. In the end she annoyed me. I suppose it was part of the diagnosing.

As it was twelve years ago, I can't recall now all of the tests.

Mum also went twice to see the psychologist. Mum was asked about the nine months, before I was born. Mum was really ill every evening, with this sickness some women get, in the first three months when they are pregnant. It just wouldn't go away.

Mum told the psychologist, how I would keep records of what I watched on video and how many times, I had seen the tape, in a book. Sometimes I would spend ages recording all of this information. When I had finished filling up the book, I would spend many hours writing all the video tapes I had bought into the next book. I would have a separate page for the U, PG, 12 and 15 rating ones. It was a bit of an obsession with me. I just had to know, how many times I had seen the video.

I suppose that I still do it now. I keep a record of all my e-books, I buy on my Kindle. How much each book is. Also how much it would be in paperback, new and used price. I can look back over my records and see how much money, I have saved by buying books though my Kindle.

EBooks are so much cheaper, than buying a hard copy. Most times they are even less than a used book. Amazon don't have to store the books, they are on some server, somewhere in the world. So that is why, they are normally so much less.

I love e-books. You don't have to wait, for your book to arrive. Less than a minute, you can download your chosen book and be reading it. Also you can have a sample of a book, before you decide whether or not, you like it enough to part with your money. No more wasted money on books, I thought I might like. Only two books in about hundred, I haven't been too keen on. I did also finish those two, they just took a little while longer to finish. They were not so bad I had to give up on them. I think that I read more now, than when I used to buy hard copies of my books.

Getting back to the psychologist, mum told her how I used to play with my cars, in a really focused manner. I wasn't into dolls and playing Mums and Dads, like most little girls are. I was more into my toy cars. I was more a tomboy than a little girl.

After Mum and I had all our tests we went for the results. It is all a bit of a blur to me what she said. She told me that I had Asperger's Syndrome, which I was shocked about. I thought that she was going to send me to see a psychiatrist. And all my problems, given time be worked though, with seeing the psychiatrist. But I have them for life. No chance of them just disappearing, one day when I wake up, they are not going anywhere. It is not nice, not being allowed to have the same chances, as the rest of the people, living in England, just because you are a little different to everyone else.

I don't think that it should have taken twenty five years, for everyone to realise what was wrong with me. After all I did go to a special needs school. And in my opinion they should have spotted it. Especially as it all went wrong at the mainstream school. If they had been keeping a proper eye on me, when I was going there, they would have realised, that there was a social problem, I was having with the other pupils, in the classroom.

Chapter 20

What Happened Next

Well nothing really, we just carried on as before.

I wasn't sent anywhere to get any help. I was just diagnosed and that was it. I had the same help as I did before, which was zero. Nobody acted any differently. The DEA at the job centre, carried on like she did before. The only difference was, that she knew what was wrong with me.

You would have thought, that I would have got more help, with finding a job. But I wasn't told about anyone who could help me. It was like, that's what is wrong with you and you've just got to get on with it. We expect you to be like everyone else, even though you are unable to understand always how you are supposed to communicate with other people you come into contact with. There are so many unwritten rules that people without Asperger's understand. It is just impossible in some situations to fit in. People don't always want to talk to you and you feel left out and not wanted. I feel that sometimes I'm in the way.

Chapter 21

Five Months Work Experience

Next the DEA sent me to this charity, who worked with people with mental and special needs problems. Neither category in my opinion, in which I fit into. But I got on well with the staff who worked for this charity, that were helping me. They treated you like a real person and were interested in finding, the right work place for me. Not just getting me off of their books and into any job, they could lay their hands on. Which the DEA tried twice to do. The washing up job and working in an old people's home. I like the elderly, but I would be unable to get that personal with them.

I went on a course, while I was there, dealing with stress. Which I can't remember anything about now. It was quite some time ago, when I was twenty six.

The charity managed to find me some work experience. In a small office for one of the biggest employees in the area. In the office there were about five of us, all sharing this one big room. We all got on well together.

I made friends with one of my co-workers. She is twelve years older than me. Has one child and lives with her partner.

My new friend showed me lots of the pubs in the town I live in. Some I never knew were there. Not that I'm a great drinker, nor is she. I had no idea how she heard of them all.

My five months there were of course un-paid. I got ten pounds extra a week, for my work there.

At the end of the five months, the lady who first saw me, managed to employ me in a paid position, but not in the small office. I had to go to their, big main open plan office. I had one of those temporary contracts for a year. My job tittle was Clerical Assistant.

Chapter 22

Paid Work

I was either twenty seven or twenty eight, when I started my first paid job.

I was so pleased that I finally had a real paid job and not just some more work experience.

I obtained this job on the new deal scheme, the government were running at the time. For the first six months, the employee received sixty pounds per week.

It took around ten years to get this job. The office was divided off into areas, where about seven people sat in each area. The dividing sections were about waist high. There were about twenty five people in our area of the open plan office. We had one side of the floor. On the other side was a different department. Around the corner was yet another different department. So about 50 people on one floor.

The department I was in, had just moved, from two or three different offices, into one big open plan office, which just left two or three, smaller offices.

So the first three months of my time, was spent helping, to unpack all of the pink boxes.

One day in these three months, the manager asked me about some file of hers that had got lost in the move. I had no idea where it could be as I was new. The other admin who I was working with me said that it probably either got destroyed or separated into different files. As the file seemed to be a really old one, from where ever she worked before. I don't know how she came to bring this file, from the job she had before, as normally you leave all files behind, when you move to a new job. None of the admin knew where this file could be. I told the manger as I was new, I couldn't find her file. But she wouldn't have it. She got a real thing about this file.

So I spent the next twenty minutes or so pretending to look for this file. I pretended to look in all the filing cabinets. I even disturbed some of the other managers, who were below this one, to look in their drawers. I made a real show, of looking everywhere. After about twenty minutes, I went back to her and told her I couldn't find her file, which she luckily accepted.

I wanted to make a good impression, so I worked really hard unpacking all of these pink boxes. It took about three months, to get the office all straight. There were so many files to unpack and find somewhere to put them all.

The first three months, I had plenty of work. My troubles didn't start until after the office was all straight.

My manager got promotion. So the next two weeks, I arranged all my own work, as I didn't have a manager. After two weeks, I felt that I should know, who my new manager was going to be. So the next two weeks, I had a temporary manager, who was really nice and understanding. It was a shame that I couldn't have kept this lady. Not that she had the power, to sort out any of my problems, as she held a lower position.

While I had this temporary manager, I was helping one of my co-workers, Sam, who was at least five grades above me, with some of her work. We were getting on well together and she seemed pleased with what I was doing.

Then one morning when I went in she was sitting opposite me, showing someone else the same job that I had been helping her out with. This went on for several days. Until in the end I got fed up with watching her work with this other person. So I complained about this to my temporary manager.

My temporary manager and I sat in a room with this lady's manager. The lady I was working with, had got into trouble for giving me this work in the first place, as it was only meant for a higher grade than I was on. Even though they were happy with what I was doing, I wasn't allowed to continue the work, so said Sam's manager.

They didn't give me something else to do. And I had to continue to watch her working with someone else, while I tried to look busy doing nothing, what so ever, which was very tiring and boring.

But later on in the year someone else had left and someone on a lower grade temporarily did that person's job. Then when the interviews came, this person got the job. So I don't see why I couldn't have helped Sam out. It wasn't as if I had other work to get on with. I'm sure this admin whom they replaced me with, had other work she could have done.

Soon after that I got a new manager. I so wish that I hadn't. She was a nightmare. Whenever I asked for work she would say go and see Sam. The only thing Sam could ever come up with was either sticking labels on leaflets, or putting packs together. My skills lay in computer work, not putting a load of packs together, sometimes it is all right, but it got so boring and tiring. I felt I could do a lot more and they were not using my skills.

One patch of leaflets I had to put labels on, had the wrong information on them, so I had to stick the right information, over the top of the wrong information. I spent several weeks doing this. I got so fed up with this. Then after a few weeks, someone decided that the leaflets, couldn't be given out, to the general public, looking like that, so they all went in the bin. What a waste of my time. I spent ages making sure they were all straight.

If I wasn't helping Sam, I would keep going to look at the photocopier to see if it needed filling with paper, or making tea for the area of the office, I was sitting in. Also, someone was collecting stamps for some sort of charity, so I would sit there cutting them off of all the envelopes that came in. I would tidy my desk up a lot, just to be doing something. Not that it needed tidying up as it didn't get used much for working on.

The first hour of each day would be spent opening the post. That was the only regular job I did each day. Occasionally I would answer the telephone and take a message, or transfer the person, to someone else.

I kept going to my manager looking for work from her. It was her job to organise my work. She had about three admins and myself to make sure, that we all had work to do. The admins always had plenty of work to do. But she never would find me any work to get on with. She just wouldn't treat me like a proper member of the team. It was always go and see Sam. It wasn't Sam's job to find me work to do. Sam would always smile at me, when she gave me some work, which annoyed me a bit. I suppose she was just being nice, but it got on my nerves. It wasn't really her fault, about what happened early in the year.

As time went on I got more and more bored. At the end of each day I would go home tired. I know that it sounds crazy. How can you be tired from doing hardly anything all day? It can be just as bad doing nothing, as being really busy.

One morning we had a power cut. I found it quite funny, as I was the only one with some work to do, as I was doing this big mail shot. I sat there watching everyone wondering what to do with themselves. After an hour or two, my manager decided that the admins, had better be doing something, instead of sitting around, so they got sent to me, to help me with my mail shot. It was my best hour or so working there. It made a change, the shoe being on the other foot, instead of mine.

In the end, I was so unhappy there, that Dad and I went back to the job centre, to see the DEA. She wasn't even slightly interested in my problems. She had me in paid employment and as far as she was concerned that was it. I said to her, "What happens if I leave, how long will it take before I can get some benefit?" "Six weeks" she said. No alarm bells went off in her head. If I had been her, I would have been more concerned, if someone was thinking about leaving their work place. I would have tried to sort out their problem, not just sit behind my desk and taken no notice of my client's problem. If I had left I would have been back on her books to sort out.

So I just had to go back and put up with the job.

In the end, I complained about not doing anything, which was in my job description, to my manager. She said that if she had been there when they had taken me on, she would had probably made my job spanning two grades, instead of one. That way I would have, I assume, then been able to do what was on my job description. The job previously had been a higher grade. A grade above mine. None of which helped me. I wasn't at all happy, as I wasn't using my skills, which lay with using the computer. There was nothing I could do about it. I just had to put up with it. It was their mistake and I was made to suffer for it. They made no adjustments for me, which I think they should have done, also they were supposed to be an equal opportunities employee. Equal opportunities I don't think really existed, it just sounds good. But if you have something which is invisible it doesn't work. They are not interested. They don't want to know. Most people only want to understand what they can see.

I continued to have this problem of not having much to do all day. Which my manager took no notice of. I kept complaining to her. In the end, she came up with this idea, for me to go around all of the managers, when I didn't have any work and see if they wanted anything doing. Which I thought was crazy and wouldn't work.

So the next time I ran out of work, I went around all the managers and asked them if they had anything, I could help them with. They all said no. Which I thought they would. I didn't try it again. It was just a waste of time. It's my manager's job to find me work to do, not all the other managers in the department. What's the matter with her? I didn't go back to her and say that I had tried her idea out. I just couldn't see the point. Looking back on it, I wonder if she was trying to make the other managers see, that there wasn't anything for me to do.

She was difficult in a subtle way. She didn't bully me out right. She also made me feel isolated from everyone else. I did talk to my temporary manager about all my problems. She was kind and listened to all I had to say. She tried talking to my manager about it all. But she said how upset she was, by what I was saying. Which I don't think she was. She just didn't want me there. All the admin staff there when I started, went on to get promotion. The replacements were employed by my manager. So I was the only old one left.

When my contact ran out, my manager changed what it said I was supposed to be doing. She took out all the bits I wasn't doing. I had no choice but to sign this six month contact. I said to her if I don't sign this, will I be out of a job. She said yes. So I reluctantly signed the new contact, which I wasn't at all happy with. I had no rights what so ever. My manger was able to do just as she liked and get away with it.

She talked to me about doing a course, where you would get a qualification at the end of it. She said that she would talk to her manager, to see if there would be any money available, for me to do this course. After a little while she came back with a no answer. I'm guessing she knew it would be a no, but it made her look good in the eyes of the other mangers above her. It looked like she was trying to help the employee with Asperger's.

They did send me on a Microsoft excel course. Which turned out to be too basic for me. I already knew everything that was being taught. So the one day course was a waste of my time. At least I had something to do that day.

My manager thought it would be a good idea for me to spend some time on reception, to see if that line of work was for me. After my three or so hours stint I was asked how it went. My replay was, I don't think it's for me. Why, I was asked? The customers coming in would annoy me. You can't really work on reception, if everyone coming in gets on your nerves. I would always be worrying about what they might want. It would worry me, in case someone came in and I didn't know the answer. That's why I wasn't that keen on answering the telephone, you never knew what you might be asked by the person at the other end of the line.

I did try for a job the other side of the office, in another department. Someone I got on quite well with, got the sack, so I applied for her job. I was a bit surprised when she got the sack. I supposed I shouldn't be all that surprised, as she did say to me one day, that she didn't think that she would be there much longer. She didn't talk to her colleagues. She was also on some sort of chat web site a lot, when she was at work. Her mind wasn't on her work, she would make silly little mistakes all the time. Her manager was really upset, that she had to sack her, as she never had to sack anyone before.

I didn't get the job. Someone else who had left, to go somewhere else and didn't get on there, got the same job back.

I also tried at the local council offices for two jobs. The interview for the lower grade job was a bit odd. It was in the electoral roll department. I had done some research before I went, so I knew who the Mayor was and how many wards were in the town.

But all my research was a waste of time, as the questions seemed to be only two answers you could give, either a yes or no. There was a lady and man doing the interviews. The man was friendly, but the lady just seemed to tolerate my presence.

I had a test afterwards. All the people in the office were friendly, it was just this one lady who wasn't.

Hence to say, that I didn't get the job.

For both interviews I disclosed that I had Asperger's.

The other interview went much better. I didn't get the job. I think my spelling let me down. But they did ring up, to tell me how impressed they were with me, which was kind and nice of them.

I decided that I would try some temping work, so that I could get some more skills to apply elsewhere. So my manager had a word with a temping agency, that the department I was in used.

I had a test with this temping agency, before I left, to see what I was able to do.

I was so glad when the job came to an end, as I couldn't stand it much longer. I had a half a week off before I started my first temping job.

Chapter 23

Temping Job

The Temping job, strangely enough was in the same building, I had been working in for the last eighteen months, on the floor below.

I was working with two other temps, who were sisters. One of the sisters, was leaving in a week's time, as she had got a permanent job elsewhere. So she had one week to train us.

All went fairly well the first week. Someone else was going to be joining us the following week, who had been there before temping, so he would know what to do.

We were packing up old files to go to a central place in England. We were cataloguing the files into the computer before they went. I felt that after the first week, the job really only needed two people.

It was the second week that the problems started. The other sister had gone to her permeant paid job and that left myself and the younger sister to work together along with this other temp.

Both temps really annoyed me. They kept surfing the internet, looking at video clips they found funny when they were supposed to be working. There were only two computers, which we took it in turns to work on. While two people were on the computer the third was supposed to be packing the files up, to be taken away later in the week.

So when it was my turn to pack up the files, I would soon run out of work. All because they both were surfing the internet, looking at these video clips in work time and getting paid for it. I was there to work, not sit looking at video clips in work time. You do that sort of thing in your own time, not while you are at work. It's just not on.

Also the temp I worked with in the first week was using my internet settings, that I had when I was working there for eighteen months, to surf the internet, which I didn't like. So after a few days had gone by, I would log out and she would have to use the other temps logging in password. He had internet access, which I didn't think temps were allowed. She never said anything to me about logging out and I never said anything to her about it. I think that they must have thought I was a bit strange, as I wanted to get on with the work I was being paid to do. We were on our own most of the week. We had been trusted to get on with the job. They just didn't seem to care. I wanted to use my time there, to gain experience which I could take into a permeant job. Temping I thought was going to help me gain more knowledge in an office which would be usefully in the future.

The person who came once a week, to see how we were getting on was a nightmare. She came every Monday morning. The first morning she came, she spent it on the phone about her car that needed repairing. All morning she was on the phone about her car. She couldn't have cared less about what we had or hadn't been doing all of last week. She was as bad as the two temps, with not doing much work. It really got on my nerves, I just wanted to get on with the work and no-one else seemed to want to. After all that was what we were being paid to do, not play on the computer doing our own thing.

After three weeks we moved to a different office to catalog and pack up some more files.

The male temp seemed to have three different personalities. One when he was with us, another one when he was working on a building site and another when it was just us. When it was just the two of us, he was nice. He would work hard and would be nice to be around.

Every Wednesday Emma would have a mood swing, you could set your clock by it. One Wednesday when she just popped out of the office, I said to the other temp, "its PMT day." He laughed. Well it was true, it was just like a woman's pre mensal tension, just before their period started. It was awful, she was so moody in the middle of every week. You could set your clock by it.

She didn't really want to be there, she was an actress, out of work, out of work actresses are called 'resting' actresses. She knew at least one of 'The Bill' cast and I think one of the 'Emmerdale' cast. She had a boyfriend who was an actor, in work. She went away most weekends to see him. It's a shame that she couldn't go away during the week, then I could have got on with the work more. She just slowed all the work up.

The person who came ever Monday morning to see us, carried on not doing much work. They started to go out in the mornings the three of them for a really long tea break. Which meant that while they were gone, I could get on with what I was being paid to do, which was work.

This Emma was away one morning and didn't get back to the early afternoon. And on her timesheet, she put that she was there all morning. She claimed for three or four hours, when she was nowhere to be seen, which didn't really sit easy with me.

I did go and have my hair cut and highlighted for about three and half hours. We had someone else come in soon after I had my hair done and they noticed it. I said "I have just had it done today." Emma said to me afterwards, that she was going to say I was there all the time, in the office, when I was at the hair dressers having it done. So I was glad that I had got in first, as I am a terrible liar and I wouldn't have wanted to lie about it. It is just not honest to claim £5.50 an hour when you are not there. I don't understand how Emma had the nerve to claim the hours when she wasn't there. If I had tried it, it would be written all over my face that I was lying.

One Monday morning when this person supposedly came to see us, about our work, she told us that she had got a job in another department, at a higher grade and more pay than she was currently on. This greatly surprised me, as I felt she wasn't doing her current job correctly. She was worried she wasn't capable of taking on this new job. Which I felt she was right to be worried about, after her performance over the last few weeks. I kept all my thoughts to myself, as it would have caused a few problems for me. I would have been the one who would have come off the worse if I had said anything to the three of them, as all three got on really well. I was the odd one, wanting to get on with the work. I was trying to gain experience, that I could write down on my C.V and hopefully gain a more fulfilling job, than the last one I had for eighteen months.

Towards the end of the six weeks we were going to go to two different offices, Emma and I to one office. Another person I think was going to be joining the other person to go somewhere else.

But I couldn't stand the thought of being alone with Emma for thirty five hours a week. I decided not to continue with this particular job.

I came in on the Monday morning, after the other two had gone to different offices, just for the morning to wait for the delivery man, to come for our files.

Chapter 24

Last Temping job and The Job Centre

A week went past, with no more temping work, so I had to sign on back at the job centre again.

I said to them about doing temping work. Would it be alright? "O yes", the man at the job centre said. So I went away happy, thinking that I could do a day here and a day there and earn a bit of extra money, with no problems, as after all I was trying to help myself.

So when another temping job came up to do a mailshot, I said "yes."

The job lasted two and a half hours. The other temp and I got paid £13.75. At the time it seemed strange, that they were saying that no one who came to them for their mailshots ever came again. I thought it was odd as well.

So the next time I went to sign on, I told them at the job centre about the work.

So when the day came for me to receive my money from the job centre, it didn't turn up. My Dad went to the job centre to find out where it was. He found out as I hadn't filled in a form about my £13.75 I had earned, it was holding up my money. But no one bothered to tell me, I was supposed to fill out a form. The man who I signed on with, should have said to me, "Have you filled the form out declaring your wages."

It was a difficult form to fill out. The form wanted to know how often you got paid and how much? How many hours each week you did? The form went on like this. With temping you might have anything from one morning's work, to six weeks or more, then nothing for a long time.

We also discovered that you are only allowed to earn £5.00. So I lost the other £.8.75 I earned. I didn't even earn the minimum wage, which back then was £5.50 an hour.

My money came two days late, when they had all the information about the £13.75 I had earned. You would have thought that I had earned over a hundred pounds for all the fuss they made over it.

I discovered about a year ago that it was still only £5.00, now the minimum wage is £6.30 per hour.

So a few more weeks went past, until the lady from the temping agency phoned me up with another mailshot job. So I explained to her why I was unable to take another mailshot job. It just wasn't worth all of the paper work at the job centre. I said that I could only take jobs that lasted for a week or more. She said that she had another job in the town centre, wrapping up other peoples Christmas presents for a few weeks. I have never been all that good at wrapping my own Christmas presents up, so I said I wasn't any good at wrapping my own up.

So that was the end of my temping days. I didn't really gain any more experience, which I hoped I would.

So I was back full time at the job centre.

Chapter 25

My Two Visits to See the DEA, at the Job Centre

So I was back to seeing the DEA. It was the same one that I had been seeing in the past, before I started the eighteen months and the six weeks temping, so nineteen and a half months paid work in all.

She said that there were these people paid by the job centre, or government to help people to get into work so she made an appointment for me to see one of them.

So Dad and I went and saw this lady in the job centre. She had this long form to fill out, which took about two hours to complete. We sat there all the two hours answering all sort of questions. None of the questions were related to my Asperger's.

At the end of it I said to her, that I had trouble thinking of the right answers at interviews. Her replay was, "I will come along with you to the interviews and make sure you understand the questions." I tried to explain to her that wasn't what the problem was. It was coming up with the right answer. I just couldn't get through to her. All she wanted to do was come along to the interview, to help me understand what was being said to me.

She said that she didn't have many computer skills, "You will be better at looking for work on the computer than me. I will make an appointment to see you in two week's time to see how you are getting on."

I wish that she had told us before we had started filling out the two hour form exercise with her, that she was going to do bugger all for me.

My Dad was upset and frustrated that this woman was not trying to understand my Asperger's at all. We just could not get through to her.

So Dad phoned the DEA up about it and another appointment was made to see the DEA.

We arrived and she wasn't at all happy with me. She went on that she had a new manager, who wasn't very happy with her, as I wasn't taking up this help, which was on offer.

Dad told her about our other interview with this lady. But all she could think about, was that she was in trouble with her new manager, which didn't help me at all. It wasn't my fault she was in trouble. She should have been having a go at the lady, who she sent me for help to, not me. I wasn't my fault that this other lady was going to cause more problems than she was supposed to solve.

Chapter 26

Change of Benefit

A few days went past, with Dad thinking where I could go from here, as the DEA was causing more problems, than she was going to solve.

In the end, Dad went to the Citizens Advice Bureau, to see what other benefits I might be able to claim. Dad was given two forms to look at, one was for incapacity benefit, the other one was disability benefit. Dad took a good look at both, then discussed it with me. The disability benefit one wasn't relevant to me as it was about washing, feeding and doing everything for the person. The incapacity benefit form was more for me. So Dad filled in the twenty or so pages for me and I signed it at the end.

I never read any of these forms as they always worry me. You feel as if you are not in control, which you are not really, the government is. I just can't stand these forms from the government. There are so many different ways to answer the questions. It's like they are trying to trip you up. Dad also finds it hard to understand what they are asking in some of the questions. It is difficult to find a correct spot, to try and get over to them how my Asperger's affects me personally. The forms are not designed for hidden disabilities.

So Dad sent the form off with the sick note from my Doctor.

Then we waited for a replay from them. Lucky they accepted my claim without any trouble. So now I don't have to go to the job centre every two weeks to sign on or see the DEA.

The DEA from the job centre did ring me up to offer some more help. I ended the call as quickly as I was able and told her that I wasn't looking for work at the moment. She didn't phone back again.

Every three months for a year, Mum and I had to go and see the Doctor to get a sick note and then sent it off, so that I could continue on the incapacity benefit. After one year, they wrote to me, to tell me that, I didn't have to go and see the Doctor and get a sick note anymore.

Which was good in one way, as I didn't have to go and see my Doctor every three months. But it also made me think, that I wasn't worth anything. I felt that they were giving up on me. I very easily feel worthless. The two paid jobs I had, had made me feel even more worthless than I already did. Not that I felt all that worthwhile before. Afterwards I felt even worse. I only told Mum this year how I felt about it. She said that she wished that I had said something at the time. But I didn't know how to express myself, and even if I did, I wouldn't have thought that Mum would be interested in, how it all made me feel.

My parents were glad that I didn't have to keep on going to see my local GP.

By this time I was thirty and we had moved into our new home.

Chapter 27

Moving House One

My parents first started to talk and think about moving, when I was twenty four. I was dead against moving house, as I couldn't imagine living anywhere else. I had lived in the same house, all my life. I could imagine being old and living in the same house. The only way I thought I would leave the house, was when I was old and died, then I would go out in a six feet long wooden box. I couldn't think about leaving any other way. I thought that I would live and die in that house, without ever moving anywhere else. I just didn't want to think or move anywhere else.

Over the next five years my parents looked at different properties on and off. They wanted a bungalow.

As my mum has an irregular heartbeat, she finds going up and down stairs tiring. The house we lived in was medium sized. It had long corridors and high ceilings. The ceiling above the stairs was sixteen feet high. Impossible for me to decorate on my own, due to how high the ceiling was. It just would be too dangerous and I don't like heights. Never have been that keen on heights. I don't know why. Nothing has ever happened to me, as far as I remember.

Also my parents were worried about me being able to look after the house, after they died. They both thought it was too big for me. I didn't agree. I liked the thought of growing old and still living in the same house.

So by the time I reached twenty nine, they got serious about moving and the house went up for sale for real this time. They had put it up for sale before, but nothing came of it. After a week or two, they would take it off the market. This time it was different, they meant business.

They stared to look for a bungalow, in a quiet part of town as both my parents don't like a lot of noise. Neither do I really.

Eventually they found a bungalow they both liked. So they took me to see it the second time, to see what I thought of it. The bungalow was in a quiet road, with only one way in and out. Houses backed onto the bungalows. The houses were in the main road. But you were far enough away, not to hear the traffic. It was a small two bedroom bungalow with a small garden. The kitchen was a bit on the small size.

We all thought we would be happy living there, so my parents made an offer on the propriety, which was accepted. We had a buyer for our house and our buyer had someone interested in buying theirs.

A few months went past. We were ready to move so was our buyer. The person we were buying from was even more ready than the rest of us, as she had to sell. But there was a problem with our buyers, buyer. He wasted everybody's time. I kept on saying to my parents, that I felt that he was a time waster. Sadly it turned out that I was right.

So our buyer's had to find another buyer for their house. It didn't take them too long to find another buyer. The Catholic Church wanted to buy their house. Which seemed really good at first. But they were so slow in getting themselves sorted out in all their paperwork.

The person whom we were buying from got fed up waiting for us. So they found someone else and said to us and the other buyer, 'whoever signs first can buy the Bungalow.' So my parents got caught up in this contract race, which they lost. They even conceded at one point in getting a bridging loan. Lucky they didn't go down that path, as they are really expensive and you have no idea how long it might take before you sell your house. They found it all very stressful.

Of course when my Dad thought he was going to lose the Bungalow he really wanted it. Before he was worried about the house opposite, where there was a lot of wood in the back garden and he wondered if they might have been running a business from there. It got a bit of an obsession of my Dad's, it drove my mum mad at times.

When we lost the Bungalow, Mum accepted that it wasn't meant to be, but Dad couldn't accept that.

Our buyer was annoyed with us in the end as we couldn't find somewhere where we wanted to live. They wanted us to move into rented housing and we wouldn't. Mum used to live in rented flats and she didn't want to again. Then they tried to offer us ten thousand pounds less, as they had found another house they liked and decided that ours was overpriced. We said 'no.' we lost our buyer!

So my parents took their house off the market and we all had a short holiday in Canterbury in Kent. My parents wanted a rest before deciding what to do next.

Chapter 28

Moving House Two

After we came back from our holiday, the house went back on the market.

The house wasn't on for long, before we had an offer, for the full price, which we accepted. She came back a few times to look. Always on Sunday morning. My Dad never met our buyer, as he went to church every Sunday.

So we started looking for a bungalow, but we couldn't find anything we liked. Dad in the end went into the estate agent who was handing the selling of our house and said, 'we are getting desperate have you got anything new.' So he said 'I have this, but it is probably too small for you.'

So we all went and looked at this bungalow.

Dad went in first followed by myself. Normally Dad would let Mum go in first. Dad and I liked the bungalow straight away. We had only been in there a few seconds and we knew we liked it. Mum said afterwards to us, that she thought, 'Well, I had better like it too, as my daughter and husband do'. But luckily Mum liked the bungalow as well. So my Dad and Mum put an offer on it, which was accepted.

It took three or four months before we moved. There was a problem with the lady buying our house, she kept wanting all sorts of different surveys carried out. She even had a video taken of the drains, as there was a manhole cover in the back garden she seemed a bit concerned about. After she got her film of our drains, she seemed satisfied that there wasn't a problem there.

You do sometimes have a manhole cover in your garden, where we are now, there is one in the front garden. It's nothing to worry about. Here we never have any trouble. In our old place, Dad sometimes had to unblock it. I suppose here we have been lucky not to have anyone putting stuff down the drain, which could cause a blockage. There were one or two younger families where we lived before. Here it is mainly older people.

The husband and wife we were buying from, got fed up waiting for us to sell our house, so they gave us a one week deadline, for Dad and Mum to sign, to buy the bungalow. Dad was all worried we were going to lose the bungalow, just like we did the last one. All because our buyer kept thinking up different surveys she wanted carried out. But it got her moving and we all signed in a matter of a few days.

A day or two before we moved the removal men came and packed everything up for us, as Mum felt it was too much for us all to pack up. We have a lot of stuff. Dad had got everything out of the roof and also had a good clear out of things. As Dad had been living in the house for forty five years, he had accumulated quite a few possessions over that time and he is a bit of a hoarder. So am I really. I still have a lot of my things in the roof, where we live now, toys from my childhood. I just can't bring myself to give them away to anyone. I don't like giving any of my stuff away. I did once give my computer away, as I was having a new and better spec computer. I gave the computer to my Mum's friend's daughter. She was very pleased with the computer, as the one she had, was about twenty years old.

On the moving day, the removal men came and took all of our belongings, out of the house and into their van. We needed two removal vans, as we had so much stuff.

The house was so empty, without our belongings in it. The rooms were so big. Not that it was a small house, the rooms were a decent size. I went around the whole house with the hover. That way I got to spend a little time in each room. I had lived there all my life. I thought that I would be still there as an old lady. I couldn't see myself ever leaving. I was only leaving, if I died in the house.

Dad didn't get all upset like I thought he was going to get. John my Mum's cousin came and helped us on the moving day, which helped a lot. Perhaps it helped Dad, Andy being there. When we closed the door for the last time, Dad didn't get upset as I thought he might.

I was also ready to move. I thought this would be new start, I can leave all my problems in the house. Leave all my troubles from the past behind me. As my life had not gone as I had hoped it would.

Chapter 29

The New Home

Our new neighbours must have wondered where all our things were going to go. I think that we wondered as well. A lot of it had to go in the garage. Dad had to leave his car out for the first few weeks, as the garage was full of some of our possessions.

Our new lounge was also full of our boxes. It took us week and weeks to unpack. The kitchen things were in the lounge for about seven months until the kitchen was finished. We were in a mess for quite a while.

For the first three or four weeks, I slept in the lounge, as the bathroom and separate toilet were the first two rooms to be decorated. I can't say that I enjoyed sleeping in the lounge as I had no space to call my own. If I wanted to go to bed, I had to wait for my parents to go first. Also I had nowhere to put any of my things. But it made more sense sleeping in the lounge, than moving my things into my bedroom, and then having to move out again so soon. It would have made more work for everyone.

But we were all on top of each other for the first few weeks. Luckily no one fell out with anyone. I did at one point think that my bedroom was never going to be started. The bathroom and separate toilet seemed to take forever to be completed. When all of your things are in three different places its gets a bit annoying.

For two nights while the bathroom was being done, we stayed at my Mum's cousin's home, as we didn't have a working toilet.

Once the bathroom and toilet were completed, a start could be made on my bedroom.

The colour scheme I choose was yellow for the walls and oatmeal for the carpet and curtains.

During my time sleeping in the lounge I had my 30th birthday. I decided that I wanted to do something different to what I normally did. Normally I do nothing what so ever. But this year I wanted to do something. So I decided to have a small champagne party. I invited my friend Brenda, who I had met while on work experience in the office. Miss Paint who I took library books to, who was in her 80's. My Mum's and Dad's two friends Marie and Dan who lived in the road we had just moved from. So in all there were seven of us. My parents bought three or four bottles of champagne.

We all sat surrounded by the boxes in the lounge and my bed was in one corner of the room. No one seemed to mind. It made it different to other people's parties. Where ever you looked in the room your eye would see a box. In one of the photos afterwards, you could see my laundry, Mum had given me to put away. For some reason, it didn't get put away before the guests arrived. I suppose that I must have forgotten about it. The room was so cluttered with some of our stuff, I don't think that anyone noticed my laundry, by the TV. If they did, they were too polite to say anything about it.

I enjoyed the party. I hadn't had one since before my tenth birthday. I had other parties when I was a child, but this was the most enjoyable one I have had so far. Miss Paint really enjoyed the party, she said that she wanted me to have one every year.

Chapter 30

Miss Paint

I first meet Miss Paint when I was eighteen. I was doing some voluntary work for the library, taking books to people who were housebound and were unable to get to the library themselves.

I would be given a list of authors and types of books the person liked. Then I would go to the library and try and find some books, I thought the person would like. Normally they would have to be in large print, as all the people I was getting books for, were in their seventies and eighties and had eye sight problems. At this time I was getting books for three ladies and Miss Paint was the third one. The books I took out, I was allowed to keep for up to three months.

Miss Paint lived on her own with her small rescued Yorkshire terrier. She did have one or two sisters and one brother, who died when she was much younger. Also one nephew. None of Miss Paint's relatives lived locally.

Miss Paint never married. She seemed happy enough living on her own.

It was a glorious summer day when I first met Miss Paint. I walked to where she lived, as she only lived about twenty five minutes away.

When I arrived, she was sitting outside in an arm chair. And I do mean an arm chair, one you sit on in the sitting room.

She invited me to sit down next to her, in another arm chair, which I did.

Miss Paint seemed pleased with the books I had picked for her. I had got three or four.

I explained how I organise seeing my other two ladies. What I did was wait until they phoned me up, to say they had nearly finished, with the books they were reading and then I would arrange another time to go and see them, with some more books. It seemed to work, for me as well as the housebound customer. You were not rushing them to finish the books in a certain time span. Sometimes there would be a longer gap in between visits, as the books had taken longer to read. Some books are thicker than others and some books you just can't get on with, no matter how hard you might try.

As time went on our relationship developed into a friendship. I would go about once a month, to see Miss Paint and take some books with me. I would stay about two hours, then walk back home.

We covered all sorts of topics from Miss Paint's trouble with her cleaners, to the existence of God. Miss Paint said that she couldn't believe in God, as why would he would let all the animals suffer in the world and not do anything about it. Miss Paint thought, if he was real, why would he let all the animals carry on suffering? She felt very strongly about this. She didn't like the way that some people treated their dogs and other pets.

At this time, I had only been going to church for a short time, so I couldn't give Miss Paint a full answer. Even if I had been able to give a full answer, I don't think it would have made any difference, as she had already made up her mind, that there was no God.

Miss Paint was a very kind lady. There was a neighbour up the road who had a son with a few problems, she would always talk to him as if he was part of the human race. Most people would not have bothered, to try and hold a conversation with this young man, but Miss Paint did.

As I said in the last chapter I invited Miss Paint to my 30th birthday party.

Mum thought, just over a year later, that it would be nice to take Miss Paint, to a local hotel for tea and a mice pie, the four of us, Mum, Dad, Miss Paint and I, as it was near Christmas. I thought that this was a nice idea and that Miss Paint would enjoy being taken out.

So Mum phoned Miss Paint up. Her nephew answered the telephone. He said that his Auntie had died. I had only seen Miss Paint, about three weeks before, this and she seemed to be in good health, but missing her dog, which she had to have put down, about two months before. Having her dog gave her a reason to get up in the mornings.

Mum said that she was sorry and could he tell us when the funeral would be held. He said that he would let us know. But we never heard anything more from Miss Paint's nephew. I would have liked to have gone to the funeral.

I had known Miss Paint for twelve to thirteen years. She even give me the pin number for her front door, if ever I needed to use it. Perhaps she was worried about laying there dead and no one knowing she was there. You hear of these stories about people who have died and not been discovered for days or weeks on end in their homes.

There may not have been a funeral, as she did say to me one day that she wanted her body to go to medical science. So she may had stipulated in her last will and testament, that she didn't want a funeral, but I wish that Miss Paint's nephew had telephoned us up and told us this. It left me thinking that he had forgotten all about me.

Chapter 31

Church

After we moved, I thought that it was time to change my life. Before we moved I hardly saw anyone or did anything much. I wanted to put the pass behind me.

I used to cycle on the seafront, three or four times a week. Also I could go on the back roads to the town, so as to avoid the main roads, which I wasn't really that happy to cycle on. What the bike cost I saved on bus fares. My Dad thought that I would never cycle enough to get my bus fares back and he also thought that I wouldn't use the bike much and that it was a waste of my money, but he was wrong. I must have saved at least twice, what it would have cost me to travel on the bus. And it is better exercise than sitting on the bus.

So a few months after we moved, Dad and I started to go to a church, a twenty minute walk away. I wanted somewhere I would be able to walk to, if I had to go on my own. I didn't want to have to pay for a bus fare, to somewhere. It all adds up when you are on benefit.

So my Mum suggested this church where she used to go to Sunday school, when she was under five years old. More than sixty five years ago.

When we got there we were welcomed by one of the members who was greeting people as they came in, who made us very welcomed. He said we have got a great new minster. We just smiled, as we knew nothing about the minster, not even his name.

Before or after the service this man came up to Dad and said "hello Ben." Dad said "hello Mr Colour." Mr Colour said call me Andrew." At first Dad had great trouble with this, as Andrew was one of the ex-head teachers in the schools, Dad used to go around. He was so used to calling Andrew Mr Colour, it just seemed too personal. Dad is more used to calling people like Andrew by their last name.

Andrew completely ignored me and didn't say a word to me, all the time he talked to my Dad. Which wasn't anything unusual for me, as it is how most people treat me. I'm just not there. It's not nice, not being there. I was so used to it, I took no notice of Andrew's behavior towards me. It was the norm for me, people talking to my parents and ignoring me.

I did ask Andrew eight years later, why he didn't say anything to me and his reply was, he thought that I didn't want to be spoken to, as I didn't look as if I was interested in what was being said. Andrew said that I was giving vibes off don't talk to me.

After the service we stayed for coffee. Two of the congregation came up to us and introduced themselves to us. A married couple in their 50's, Linda and Des. They were very friendly and for the first time I was treated the same as my Dad. They didn't just talk to my Dad and not me. Which was new to me, as people normally take no notice of me.

It made me want to go back the following Sunday. First impression are very important. If no-one had been friendly towards me, I may have not gone back the following week.

Chapter 32

Driving Lessons

While I was at work I had some driving lessons, with two different people that didn't work out.

The first one was the worst one. He was a man that worked on his own. He would always wear the same clothes. I never saw him in any other clothes. He was always on about dying during your lessons, which was rather off putting. I didn't want to hear about dying in a car, while I was learning how to drive.

After I stopped having lessons with him, I discovered I wasn't the only one he went on to about dying. Someone else had a son about two years old at the time and he would keep saying to her your son could have been in that car, in front and you could have killed him. In the end she also went to someone else and in the end passed her driving test.

Our ex-neighbours daughter had some lessons with him and one of the lessons, they went to a nearby car park and he just sat there talking for the hour that she was supposed to be learning to drive.

So it wasn't anything that I did, to upset him, as other people had also had some trouble with this particular driving instructor. Also my driving instructor was very nosy. One lesson I was driving and he started to ask questions about my friend's mother, which I was trying to avoid answering, as I didn't think it was any of his business. In the end he said "Has she got two heads your friend's mother?" "No", I said. So I had to tell him that she was gay. He said in a big loud voice, really, really, really, and moving around in his seat in an excited manner. I didn't want that when I was trying to get used to driving a car. He acted like my friend's mother, was the only gay person in the whole of England. I didn't say anything to him, as I was so taken aback by his reaction and all the noise he was making next to me. Plus I wouldn't have known what to say to him. It put me off my driving.

One of my lessons was an hour before I went to work. He decided, that I wasn't learning to drive as fast as he thought that I should be, so he had a go at me for learning too slowly in his opinion. I wasn't too happy, as I think that everyone learns at a different pace. Some learn to drive really quickly, others like myself take much longer. I hadn't told him that I had Asperger's, which may have had an effect on the speed, which it took me to get used to the car and roads. I was paying him for the lessons, so what did it matter, that I was taking longer to pick it up. I was alright in work that day.

I had one more lesson with him after that. I was so glad when the lesson was over, as I was feeling a bit ill, by the end of it. He dropped me around the corner from where I lived.

By the time I got home, I felt even more ill. I went straight to the loo. I couldn't breathe properly, I thought that I was dying, so I called for my mum, but she didn't hear me as she was out in the garden. I was unable to get up and go to my mum, as I couldn't stand up and move much. So that made me panic more and have more difficulty in breathing. I really thought that I was going to die, in the loo. I thought this is it. In the end it passed off. Afterwards I was really cold, so mum put me to bed with a hot water bottle even though it was summer.

I realised afterward that what I had was a panic attack.

So I had a three week rest from learning to drive.

The next driving instructor, didn't go on about dying. But I worked five days a week. So the only time, I was able to have lessons was at the weekend. I wanted a lesson in the afternoon. The driving instructor didn't work Sundays. So the only slot he could offer me was Saturday mornings. So I had my lessons Saturday mornings. But there was a problem, the driving instructor kept having Saturdays off. So each time I had a lesson, I had to re-cap on what I had already learnt. I found it hard to move on with the lessons.

After a few months I thought I have had enough of this, it's costing me a fortune in money to learn to drive. So I gave up. Three years later we moved.

It wasn't so easy to get into town on my bike, as it was before, I couldn't go on the back roads to town, as there were none. I had to go on the main roads, which Dad wasn't too happy about. Or it was up and down on the pavements, which you are not supposed to do. I did it once or twice, but I got fed up having to keep stopping at the end of the pavements and going down, then up the other side, it took for every to get into town. And I didn't enjoy the cycle ride. I did try the main roads a few times, but I didn't feel all that safe. As cars would drive sometimes too close to me and I was worried about being knocked off my bike by them.

So I started my driving lessons again. This time I wanted to learn on a Mini, one of the new ones on the road. So I managed to find a driving school where all the cars were Minis. The price wasn't bad either, cheaper than it was when I tried to learn three years early.

My new driving instructor didn't like to go on holiday, his wife went on her own with the children to Spain. That's how much he disliked to go away. All the nine months it took me to pass, he never had a day off work. Not even a few days to go out with his wife and children somewhere for the day. The only hobby he seemed to have was table tennis. He didn't seem to do anything else in his spare time.

He knew when to be quiet and when to talk, not like my first driving instructor who would keep on talking. Also he was very calm and didn't get upset with me for taking longer to get the hang of driving. I didn't tell him that I had Asperger's, as I was worried that it might put him off from teaching me, or that he might treat me like an idiot. Also I thought that it might make him nervous about being in the car with me.

It is a constant concern of mine, what people will think of my Asperger's and how they will treat me, if they find out that I have it. I feel that some people will think that you are an idiot. I'm not an idiot. Some people with Asperger's I know have degrees. One person worked in the police force and got quite high up in it. He wasn't diagnosed until after he retired.

I got on really well with my driving instructor. Even now I see him about town, teaching someone to drive. He waved at me the other day, after seven years of not seeing me, when I was driving around town. I must have left an impression on him, for him to remember me after all this time. Seven years is a long time.

I used a computer program to practice for the theory test. You had to get thirty one out of thirty five to pass the test. The most I got while practicing was thirty one. On the real test I got thirty two right. One more than when I was practicing.

On my first go for the driving test I had to open the bonnet up on the car. It took me ages to open the bonnet, my driving instructor was in the back of the car. He kept saying out of the side of his month right, right, right, I thought what is he trying to tell me. Afterwards I realised that he was trying to tell me where the catch for the bonnet was. Also I had to read a number plate, I couldn't read the European one as the writing on it was narrower than the UK one. I said, 'I can see the UK one'. So I was allowed to read that one instead. By the time I got to leave the test centre everyone else had been gone about five minutes. We got about one hundred meters from the test centre and the examiner said 'can you put the hand break down please.' I thought, "Oh no", I failed even before I have got to the end of the road. Which I had.

After the test I thought that I had better get my eyes tested, as I had trouble reading the number plate during the test. There wasn't anything wrong with my eyes. He said that it was most likely nervous blindness. Which was a relief, as I didn't want to have to wear glasses at my age.

The second time I was asked to go out of the parking space, then to back into it and park the car. It took me five go's to get it right.

Dad was in the test centre waiting room watching me from the window, going in and out five times in this space. There was another driving instructor in the waiting room with my Dad, he said to my Dad 'don't worry your daughter will pass.' Luckily I couldn't see my Dad watching me, as it would have made me even more nervous than I already was. Dad thought I was going to fail, even before I left the test centre. Everyone else was long gone, by the time I got driving down the road.

But the chief examiner passed me. My driving instructor said that I drove better the last time on my test, than this time, when I passed. My Dad thought that I would never pass, as he thought that I was not aware enough, of the other cars on the road. But I was determined to get my driving license.

Chapter 33

My First Homegroup in the Church

About eight months after I joined the church, the church did a study which everyone who was in a homegroup took part in. At the time Dad and I were not in a homegroup. So we joined one for the study which was supposed to take six weeks, for once a week.

Homegroups are a few people meeting together normally in someone's home to study the bible. In size they can be just three or four people. Our church prefers the groups to be not more than eight people. Then everyone in theory, should be able to get to know each other and to be able to support one another. Also it should make it easy to take part in the meetings.

Neither Dad nor I got much out of the homegroup. Our hosts were not very welcoming and quite rude each week. It was a group of eight people. Dad and I didn't know anyone in the group. Each week when we arrived, four of the group would talk about people that Dad and I and two others of the group didn't know. We would sit like the four stooges waiting for the meeting to get underway. Us four were very quiet, so we found it hard to talk to one another. We would just sit there, waiting for the others to stop talking.

One evening while I was upstairs in the bathroom. Amber who later became a friend, was sitting down stairs with my Dad and one of our host. Amber was a fan of Harry Potter and watched all the films. She was talking about the films and our host had a go at her for watching it. He didn't like it, as he felt it was evil as magic was used in the films.

Later on in the evening, Amber mention to everyone, what he had said early on. He said "no I didn't say that." Dad said "yes you did." He did say then "did I say that." Dad said "yes you did." He did then say that he was sorry.

Each week our hosts wanted the meeting at their house, as they had two young children. Nobody minded this. But the husband would complain most weeks how hard it was for his wife, to get the house clean and ready for us all each week.

Each week at the end of the meeting we all would have a tea or coffee. About the third week in, the meeting was coming to an end and the husband said "you all have to go now as my wife is very tired." So we all stood on the door step for about half a minute wondering what to do, before we all departed for our cars. Dad and I both felt it was so rude of him, to just tell us all to go now. No sorry or anything. It was so abrupt, one minute we were all sitting in the lounge, the next we all were standing on our host door step.

The rest of the meetings we had our tea or coffee, when we arrived. That way we all left straight after the meeting and didn't linger and tire out, our un-friendly hosts.

If it was so much trouble each week, to hold the meetings in their house, I don't know why one of them went to one homegroup, while the other stayed behind and looked after the children. Then the other one could have gone somewhere one of the other nights.

Another thing that annoyed my Dad was that the husband would keep going on, about his son who wasn't very bright, but his daughter was. In the end Dad said to him "that he should be grateful, that his son was fit and well and had no health problems. " After that, he never went on about, what he thought his sons short coming were.

We were all supposed to have a project in each of our homegroups which would help the community in some way or other. So our group discussed going to one of the local schools and painting the climbing frames and other staff in the playgrounds. One of our host was really interested in doing this, more than the rest of us were. But the following week, he had gone completely the other way and said he just didn't have the time, to do any project what so ever. So our group never did anything. One week out of the six we missed and never did. It didn't bother me, as I wasn't enjoying my experience in my first homegroup.

I was so glad when the study came to an end. So was Amber and my Dad. The three of us left the group at the end of it.

Chapter 34

My First Car

After I passed my driving test it was time to get my first wheels. I didn't want to wait long. Dad wanted me to wait, as he didn't want me to buy a car, as he thought that I wouldn't be safe on the road. It didn't matter to my Dad that I had passed my test and that the examiner thought that I was safe. He just thought that I wouldn't be aware enough of the other cars on the road, to be out driving around. Also that I would not be able to afford the cost of running a car.

So I looked in the Friday add for a used car. I found one that I thought might be suitable for me. A small blue Nissan Micro, eight years old, with a sun roof.

So the three of us went for a test drive, Dad, John my Mum's cousin and myself. John thought it was ideal for me, as I only wanted a small car, that wouldn't cost too much to run and would be easy to park.

So I said "yes", to the car. Dad wasn't so pleased, as he wanted me to have another Micro, which was there, which was two years younger than the blue one. But I said "no, as it was seven hundred more pounds and I didn't have seven hundred more pounds." Dad got quite persistent about me buying the yellow one, as it was two years younger. Dad never in all his life, bought a car that was eight years old. To him it was just too old, to even consider to buy. It also seemed to Dad, to have a lot of miles on the clock, seventy eight thousand miles. But it was all I could afford. As it was, my parents lent me five hundred pounds, to buy the eight years old car. I was going to pay them back eight pounds once every two weeks. But it didn't work out, as I needed the money to run the car. So I only managed to pay them back, twenty four pounds. So my parents let me have the rest as a gift.

The car insurance for the first year, was really dear over six hundred pounds, as I had the zero excess, as I had no spare money if I needed to make a claim. Luckily I didn't need to make a claim, until seven years later.

So two weeks after I passed my test, I had my little blue car, with a sun roof. It's a special edition micro 1998, the model is called 'alliy'. I liked it.

The first two weeks I was really nervous, as I was used to having a driving instructor sitting next to me. Dad wouldn't come out with me, as he didn't think I should be out on the road, even though I had passed my test. But as time went on, I got used to being on my own in the car. Now seven years on, he thinks I am a good driver. Dad even now lets me drive his car. Sometimes I take his car out on my own.

Chapter 35

Homegroup Two

Dad and Amber went to a different home group to me. I did try the same group to see if it would suit me, but it just wasn't right for me. Straight away when you got in the door everyone wanted to hug you. I don't like to be hugged. There is only three people allowed to hug me, my parents and Andrew. I come to Andrew in a later chapter. Also they were just so loud. It was just too much for me. They made me feel welcome, just a bit too much for my comfort zone. I like people to keep their hands off of me, not on me.

So I joined a quieter homegroup. Three of the group were students who had come to learn English. Two from South Korea and one from Germany. The one from Germany, wanted to be a missionary, in North Korea. It is one of the most challenging places to be a Christian. You get sent to jail and mistreated. It is one of the most difficult places in the world to live in, if you are a Christian. There were about seven of us in the group. I was in this homegroup for a year, to one and a half years.

Things started to go all wrong, when the students had finished their studies and all went back home. New people came into the group. Two I had never seen in the church, but everyone else in the group seemed to know them really well. It was like I had been away for six months and come back and no one bothered to say who they were to me. Straight away after these two had joined, we couldn't have the meeting for two weeks in the house we normally did, as the leader of our group, wasn't going to be there, so we were going to have it in these new people's house, who everyone apart from me knew. I thought I can't go there. So for the next two weeks I didn't go. And quite frankly I preferred to be at my art group, which was on the same night. The group just wasn't the same after the students left. I didn't fit in and I didn't feel all that welcomed any more.

I went one more time and it just got worst for me. Also that night I had trouble with one of the neighbours about where I had parked my car. The house was in a close. Outside the house was a big green, like a roundabout. Everyone who lived there parked their car around the green. Normally the pavement side. But this night I thought I would be in the way so I parked my car nearer the green. But someone else came along after I had parked my car and parked their car opposite mine on the pavement side and caused the road to be blocked. I got the blame for blocking the road. One of the neighbours put a note on my car complaining to me where I had parked my car. I was so mad, if I could have worked out who wrote the note, I would have put it though their letter box. Instead I tore it in dozens of little pieces and put it in a skip and then got in my car and went home. I didn't tell my homegroup leader, about the note on my car. I doubt that she would have been all that interested in it.

I spoke to my homegroup leader and said that I was leaving and going to join the same homegroup, which my Dad was in. By this time I had got to know them some more, they still knew that I didn't like to be hugged. She seemed way too pleased for my liking that I was leaving her group. I felt that she was worried, that I wasn't going to cope, with the new bible studies, we were having, as they were not as easy as they were before and that she was glad, that someone else, had the worry of me instead and that it wasn't her worry anymore.

Sometimes when I talk to her, I'm wondering what she is thinking about me. I don't think she thinks I'm all there.

Chapter 36

Art Group

When I was at school I had no interested in art what so ever. I just found it boring. The teachers didn't try and teach it.

A few months after going to the church, I made a friend there who was into drawing and painting. I first met Amber in the homegroup Dad and I were in. She went to an art group run by one of the church leaders, this Andrew whom my Dad knows. She kept on to me about coming along. I kept on saying no to her, as I wasn't interested in art. In the end she wore me down and I agreed to go, just so she would stop going on about it. They were a small friendly group. About four from the church went and about four from outside. You just took your own paints along and did your own thing, no-one was there telling you what to do. We would sometimes have someone come in to give us a lesson. Either for the evening, or once we had someone in for the whole day.

I started off with painting by numbers, which I never finished, as I soon went onto painting my own pictures. The painting by numbers is still down by the side of my computer desk unfinished.

My first real painting was of some beach huts, which I did at home to see if I was able to paint and that I liked painting. I painted the beach huts in acrylics with some cheaper paint that I bought from the supermarket. I bought three or four brushes and watercolour paper from Sussex Stationers. I didn't buy the more expensive paper which the lady in the shop recommended as I wasn't sure if I was going to like painting. All the painting equipment cost around fifteen pounds. My mum kindly gave me half of the money towards all the painting materials that I needed to get me started.

One of the art group members, ran two other groups elsewhere in town.

If you got stuck with your painting she was the one to go to for advice, on what you could possibly do with your picture.

She was quite often trying to give Andrew advice on not using white goulash with his watercolours. Helen said that it made his paintings look chalkier. I don't think that he agreed, as the following week he would get his white goulash paint out and put it into his watercolours. He would do this most weeks. It gave me some entertainment, watching Helen and Andrew each week. Helen just wouldn't give up on trying to stop Andrew.

Chapter 37

My First Art Exhibition

In 2009 the art group that I belonged to, thought that they would have an art exhibition. Anyone from the group was allowed to hang up their paintings. So I decided to hang a few up, one was of two cats on some pink pots in acrylics. So I went to a shop that sells frames and mounts, to choose ones that I thought went well with my paintings. I bought about five or six frames and mounts. Over the next few weeks, I framed my own paintings. To get them professionally framed would have cost a lot more, at least three times more. Everyone else from the art group framed their own paintings, no one had them framed by a professional framer.

We held the art exhibition over one and a half days. All day Saturday and Sunday afternoon, as the church held their service where we were hanging our paintings, so they needed the area in the morning. The paintings were still up, but the stands had to be pushed up against the walls, so that the chairs could all be put out. But it did mean that some of the church, would look at our paintings and Andrew and myself were there to sell them, to anyone who was interested, in buying them after the service.

A few weeks before the exhibition Andrew said to me 'you might not sell anything the first time.' Which I didn't at the time think was very encouraging. It's like telling you, you are no good and that you shouldn't bother to put up any of your paintings. Luckily I took no notice of Andrew and hanged my paintings up with everyone else's from the group, as I didn't think they were all that bad. Not that they were wonderful either. Helen and Penny's paintings I thought were a lot better than mine.

But looking back on Andrew's words now, I think what was in his mind, was that he didn't want me to think, that I would sell, some or all of my paintings and then be disappointed that no-one had bought anything. But I wasn't thinking that I would sell all or even one of my artwork. I was hoping that I would sell one, as everyone else was, but you never know, when you display your artwork, if you will get anyone who likes your paintings. Sometimes it's the right person, coming along at the right time, and if they don't come along you won't sell. The art market can be funny. What one person likes someone else can't stand.

We all took a turn helping out at the exhibition. I went twice and helped.

Ginny, one of the people who goes to the church came along and looked at the art work. She bought my cats on the pink pots, which I was ever so pleased about. Ginny's Mother likes cats, so she bought the painting to give to her as a present. My parents were so pleased that I managed to sell a painting, as it was the first time, anyone had seen my art work. After commission, I received around thirteen pounds, as some of the money, I received from selling my art work, went to charity. After all of the framing costs I didn't make any money, although I had sold a painting. I would have to have sold at least two of my paintings, just to break even.

Chapter 38

Andrew

I first meet Andrew when I went to the church. He was dead unfriendly towards me which I wrote about in an early chapter.

I've been going to the church for a while and didn't feel I was getting on all that well in the church, I was going ever Sunday morning, but I still wasn't anywhere near close to knowing God. God was still this very, very, distance man that I didn't know. Andrew unfortunately for him, did this sermon and at the end of it he said something like, if anyone wants help in getting to know God please either speak to me or someone else. I went away and thought about this, as I was thinking about writing a letter to the leaders and asking them for some help. So the following week I took a letter along and at the end of the service, I gave my letter to Andrew asking him if I could see him. I think that he was a bit surprised, that I would go up to him and give him a letter, as up to this point, I hardly had spoken to him.

A week or two later Dad and I went to his house. I had a list of questions that I wanted answers to. I can't remember many of them now. The ones that I do remember, I'm not sure if I did ask them now, as it was about eight years ago. So I won't write any of them down, just in case they are wrong.

I was ever so nervous about going to see Andrew, as my Dad had talked about Andrew, as the ex-headmaster of one of the best schools in the town we lived in. That was back when Andrew was running the school, but now he's retired and the school is not so good, but they are now trying to improve things. Dad said that sometimes when he went he could hear Andrew shouting from his office at one of the children. So it was an odd choice of mine to want to go and see Andrew, as I was and still am a bit of a nervous person. Andrew is two years older than my Dad.

We were there for around two hours going over all of my questioners. Andrew didn't seem to mind me asking a lot of my questioners that I wanted to ask. Before I left Andrew gave me a new testament to read and we made another appointment for me to go back in a couple of weeks, this time on my own.

Two weeks time I went back on my own to see Andrew. I was a bit early 15 minutes, as I didn't want to be late. I had to wait until his other visitor went. By the end of my visit, I was tired from all of the concentrating, I had been doing, trying to take in everything Andrew was trying to say to me. As time went on and I got to know Andrew more, I wasn't nervous of him anymore. I think now my dad is more nervous of Andrew than I am. I now see Andrew once a week. Sometimes Andrew asks me to help him with his tablet or stuff on his computer. Most of the time though Andrew is helping me. In the past I have asked for some Math's lessons, as I wasn't taught very well at school. The last three years the school just didn't bother. Now Andrew is checking my life story for me and correcting any spelling mistakes and my grammar for me. Over the years we have become good friends.

Chapter 39

Atos

After eight years of being on incapacity benefit, I was suddenly sent a form to fill in, about twenty pages long. I had one month to fill it in or lose my benefit. Any form from the benefit people worries me. Dad fills all my forms in for me, as I find them too stressful. I just sign them at the end, I don't even read what Dad writes on the form, it would just worry me too much.

After about two months I had to go and see them, Dad came with me. My appointment was half an hour late, due to them being a Doctor down. I found it stressful sitting there waiting and waiting then waiting some more. I ended up spending a penny twice while I waited with my Dad.

Dad came in with me. We were in there about thirty minutes. Unbeknown to me at the time I fell into all the traps set for me. One of the questions was have you been on holiday this year. I had been on holiday to Venice in May with Andrew's wife. My Dad was supposed to go with me, to support me, but my Mum's health wasn't very good at the time, so Andrew's wife came for five days to support me, as I wouldn't have been able to go. We didn't think to tell this lady from Atos that she was there to support me. At the time I didn't relies it was relevant.

Also I tried to avoid telling her, that I had a driver's license, as I felt that they might think it made me normal. But somehow she guessed that I could drive. So that was another trap that I fell in. It doesn't mean just because you have a driver's license that there is nothing wrong with you. People drive who have all sorts of different things wrong with them. My Asperger's is communicating with people face to face, nothing to do with my ability to drive a car. The two are completely unconnected with each other, but I don't think that was what she thought.

She asked me at the end if there was anything that I wanted to add, but I couldn't think of anything. I thought that I should add something, but nothing came to mind. I did ask Dad if he could think of anything to add, but nothing came to his mind either.

Within about six weeks I had lost my incapacity benefit. Someone said that the appeals process was very stressful, so I decided not to go down that path.

Chapter 40

The Job Centre for Three and a Half Months.

I left it for as long as possible before making an appointment to see someone at the Job Centre. Dad went with me to make my claim. The lady we saw was nice to me and seemed to understand that I had a problem. She said normally you have to say that you will look for work up to ninety minutes away from where you live, but as I had Asperger's she would make it forty five minutes. Also you were supposed to fill out a form and take it with you every time you went. On the form you were supposed to put down four things you had done during the week to look for work. She said that I could put down just three things. The times for going were between 10am in the morning until 4pm. Each time you went it would be a different time. Which didn't really suit me, as I would have liked it to be the same time every two weeks. That way you know where you are. My Dad thought that it was to make it harder for you to do a job and try and claim benefit at the same time.

I was so glad when I could get away from the Job Centre as it had changed so much from the last time I went. On the door there now is about three or four security men, who asked you what you are there for. You get this each time you go. Just getting pass them, I found daunting for the three and a half months that I went. The security men were just like the bouncers you get outside nightclubs, it un-nerved me every time I went.

Then you have to go up to the desk and say why you are there, which I did with my Dad, apart from the first time when Andrew went with me.

The first time I went Andrew came with me, as my Mum had a hospital appointment in London, that was the worst time at the Job Centre. Once we got passed the front desk we had to go and sit down in the main job centre and wait to be called over to a desk. Each time you went you were supposed to see the same person.

Mr N called me over and Andrew went with me and we sat down. I gave him my form and he wasn't at all happy with it. I was about to start a course for people with Asperger's about helping them get into work. It was for about 10-12 weeks for two hours once a week. It was a forty five minute drive away. He dismissed my course as un-important and not relevant to me finding work. Also I did two and a half hours of voluntary work, at the church I went to, each week in the office. That was wrong. I tried to explain to him about my Asperger's and he just wasn't interested. Mr N dismissed it, he just didn't want to know anything about it. I said to him about seeing the disability employment advisor and he said there was probably a two month wait, before I would see this person. Mr N said that they didn't always finish their appointments at 4pm and that I might have to come later, which I didn't like the sound of.

At this time I was taking piano lessons ever Wednesday for half an hour at 16.30, so I told him about it and that annoyed him. Everything I said annoyed him. What did he expect me to have done for the last eight years? All he wanted me to do now, was sit 24/7, looking for a job and nothing else what so ever. The last eight years I have been trying to make a life for myself the best way I could, which at times was not easy.

By the time we got outside Andrew could see that I was upset, so he invited me back to his bungalow, for a cup of tea, before I went to my piano lesson.

It wasn't until I got back after my lesson to the empty bungalow that I broke down. Mum had left me my tea all made, but I was too upset to eat any of it. The thought of having to go there for the next thirty years and seeing this Mr N every two weeks, filled me with horror. At the best of times I didn't like the Job Centre, but it had never been anything like this. He just psychologically bullied me in the few minutes that I was there. So by the time my parents came back I was a mess. I had been crying for over two hours and mum, after having been in London all day, had to spend time talking to me. Dad said that he would ring the disability employment advisor the next day and that was what Dad did and I had an appointment with him in two weeks' time. So all that stuff about two months was a load of rubbish.

The DEA was nice and understood and could see where I was coming from and was really happy with what I was doing. He was happy with this course I was on and the voluntary job I was doing at the church. He was so different to My N.

But I still found it stressful going, I could never speak to the lady on the desk, when you went in and had to say why you where there, my Dad used to have to talk to her. Then you would have to walk the full length down stairs and pass Mr N, then up some stairs, to the first floor and talk to the security man on the desk and say again why you were there. So three times in all, you had to say what you purpose was in being there. I found just getting to the DEAs office stressful. For the three and a half months that I went I had trouble sleeping and was tired all the time and couldn't keep still in my bed when I was trying to get off to sleep. It was on my mind all the time going to the Job Centre, it was so depressing. There was no point in going to the Job Centre, as I don't think there was any chance of getting a job, 0% percent chance of anyone employing me. Number one I have Asperger's. Number two, I went to a special needs school. Number three, I had been out of work, at this point for eight years. So everything was against me.

Chapter 41

Andy's Help with Benefits

By the time Christmas came, I could not stand it any longer, going to the Job Centre. So Andy who ran the Asperger's Support group in the beginning, started an appeal for me. He took a close look at all my paperwork and discovered that the person who accessed me back in the summer, wasn't a Doctor but a Nurse Disability Specialist. You are led to believe, when you go to these assessments, that they are all Doctors and know about your condition, which just isn't true.

More times than I can count, while I was waiting to hear, if I had won my appeal, I just wanted to be dead. I just wanted to get cancer and die so that it would all be over with, as I was convinced that I was going to loose and I couldn't go back to the Job Centre as I couldn't cope with going there. I was just going to live off my parents and be a burden to them both. The waiting was terrible. A whole year of waiting to hear from them. It got that ever brown envelope that came though door I had trouble picking up without shaking, as I was afraid of what they might say. The benefit people always use brown envelopes. Andy had loads of correspondence with them. During the year Mum and I went and saw the Doctor and asked her if she would be willing to write me a letter, supporting the fact that I was unable to work, which she agreed to write. Andy used this letter from my Doctor in his appeal for me. We did have to pay for this letter. Eventually they admitted that the interview I had had with this Nurse, hadn't been done correctly, and that I had won my appeal, to go on Employment Support Allowance. There are two groups, the work related group and the support group. I am in the support group. The work related group you are supposed to be working towards getting back into work.

Without Andy's help I would now be without any money. So as a family we will always be grateful, for all his help and support and understanding.

Over a year later I still don't feel that I have recovered from my three and a half months of going to the Job Centre, and the whole year of just waiting. While I was waiting I tried to get a year's supply of toiletries. Each time I went to the local supermarket I would come back with something. I must have talked to Andy at least three or four times about buying toothpaste. Even now they could write to me, wanting to see me, as they review it between three months and three years and you just don't know, when they might write to you. So you are always waiting.

I kept worrying about what would happen to me after my parents died, and all the money had gone. I thought that I must time the running out of money just right so that I still had a roof over my head. I didn't want to live on the streets while I waited to die of hunger. I wanted to starve to death in the warm!

Chapter 42

Asperger's Support Group

When I first went to the support group, the group had been running for three or four weeks. Andy was running the group. There were about five of us going in the beginning. Helen from the two Art groups I go to told me about the support group, she had seen it advertised in the local paper and thought it might help me, as she went to one for her Crones disease for about twenty five years. The group was once a week for two hours on a Friday afternoon. I had never been to a support group before, so I didn't know what to expect from attending the group.

What struck me in the first week or two of going, was that I was not the only one in the whole wide world with Asperger's, that there were other people with it. You feel in the end that you are all on your own with having the condition and that no one else understands or wants to understand, the world just wants you to fit in with how it runs. I know that might sound a bit strange to people who don't have Asperger's. It's like it is the world and me.

All ages go to the group the youngest eighteen to about fifty two years old. From all walks of life. One person who came for awhile worked aboard a lot as he found that he got on better with the people as they just thought he was a bit different as he was from England. He would go for three or so months at a time, and where ever he was working they would provide an interpreter for him, who would go around with him. He once had around two thousand people under him. This person never told the people who he worked for that he had Asperger's.

Another member of the group didn't find out that he had Asperger's until he took early retirement from the police force. He didn't find out until he was in his fifties. Mr DM said that he used to find it hard to get on socially with his work colleges. Sometime Mr DM would have a bit of conflict with other people he worked with. He got quiet high up in his job. I personally think that his Asperger's helped him in his job. I think that he probably noticed things about some cases which other people might have missed.

Apart from one person, all the others who are going now are different. In the three years that I have been going, there have been a lot of comings and goings of people to the group. There has been about eighteen to twenty five people in the time I have been going.

One person who is going at the moment, I remember from my time at college when I was sixteen. At first I thought he was this boy from school, who kept being told by the teacher to take out his hands from his trousers pockets.

It's good for me to spend some time each week with people who have some of the same problems as me, you don't feel so on your own.

About three or four of the group members are graduates. One has a degree in the Arts another in speaking Italian.

Chapter 43

The Table Sale

One of the members of the Asperger's Support group thought it would be nice to raise money so we could have a day out. This person came up with having a table sale and some members of the group donated items they no longer wanted which were kept in his garage until needed for the sale. Over the coming weeks, there was a lot of discussion on where we might have this sale.

In the end, the Mother of this person helped to organise where it took place and managed to get permission from the manager of the sheltered housing where she lived to hold our group's sale in the residents lounge. It took quite some organising, deciding on what date would suit most people who would be manning the tables, and I think in the end we had three long tables. The person who ran the support group came and helped, not Andy as his boss had got promotion and he was needed more in the office, so he couldn't go out and about as much as he did before, which he told me he missed. So Tony came and helped, as I suggested that I thought it best that someone else apart from us, looked after the money. Everyone seemed to think that was a good idea.

The afternoon of the sale eventually came and most who said that they would help came along. About eight or nine in all. One person helped in the Kitchen serving tea and coffee whist the rest of us were in the lounge putting the things on the tables for sale. Four of us, including myself, stood or sat behind the tables selling the donated items to people who lived in the sheltered housing, as it was only allowed to be advertised internally and members of the public were not allowed to come in. By the end of the afternoon we had sold around ninety pounds worth of items including the teas/coffees and cakes which also went down well.

I really quiet enjoyed the afternoon working with my fellow group members. As I don't normally spend much time with them outside of the group. We all got on well. I think Tony was surprised how well it all went, as I don't think anyone else had done anything like this before.

In the end the money wasn't used for a day out, it went towards going out for a Christmas meal. Most people who helped with the table sale, did go for the meal, about two didn't I think, one of them was busy and couldn't make it, and the other person I don't know why he didn't come.

Chapter 44

My Dad Not the Stanger Anymore

Before I was diagnosed with having Asperger's, my Dad just thought that I was lazy and difficult. But afterwards he started to realise that there was more to me than he thought, for the last twenty five years. Once he realised there was something wrong with me and I wasn't trying to be difficult and lazy, Dad started to take the time to get to know me. But he will never be able to make up for the twenty five years, where he didn't bother with me and only noticed me when I was doing something he thought wasn't right.

Now we spend some quality time together each week. On Friday nights we either stay in and watch a film and share a bottle of wine, or go to two different pubs for a drink. Twice a month on a Friday we go and watch a local art demonstration as we both belong to two local art societies which have a demo once a month. After the art demo we normal go to a pub and have a drink before we go home.

On Monday's I go to an art group in the mornings, which my friend Helen runs. Dad has been going for just over a year with me. Mum and I thought it would be good for him, as Dad doesn't see many people outside of the church, since we moved just over nine years ago, Dad has been going to church and not mixing with any other people, which Mum and I thought wasn't good for him, as we both think it isn't all that healthy for him. We feel that some people in the church are talking advantage of Dad's good and kind nature and keep asking him to do little D.I.Y jobs for them. A lot of the time there is a lot of running around in the car to get the right stuff to carry out this work. My Dad finds in really difficult to say no to people, he likes to be liked more than most people do. He's afraid to offend people by saying no. Also he finds it hard to ask people for money for the stuff he has bought. A few times he has paid out of his own pocket to do jobs for other people, as he didn't like to ask them for money. I have said to Dad to say to them, "here is the receipt, then they will pay you your money", but he is so worried about upsetting the person that he would rather be out of pocket himself.

It drives my Mum around the bend Dad keep saying yes to people. Mum can't get her own jobs done. We have been in a new place now, for just over nine years and Mum still is waiting for things to be done here. Mum would also like to see more of my Dad and go out and have tea and cake with him. When he is home Dad is catching up on little jobs everyone has to do at home, to keep a place running and clean.

To me Dad seems to take longer doing everything than everyone else. I do feel that the way that he has carried out his life, that he does have Asperger's, Dad doesn't think so.

Dad does look after my Mum well when he is not driving her mad. Mum has a few health issues. She has an irregular heartbeat, and other heart problems plus spondylitis, which make it hard for her to do a lot as she gets tired very quickly.

Chapter 45

My Hobbies and Other Things That I Enjoy

A friend plays a lot of these hidden object games, I did try one about ten years ago and wasn't all that impressed with it, so I didn't bother at the time to try another one. But three years ago I thought I would try another one. Just in-case you are wondering what a hidden object game is, it can be like a point and click game, but with scenes within the main gameplay where you have to find objects. You may have to look at a close up of a desk to look for a list of items, to be able to proceed in the game. Some hidden object games don't have a story line, it just about looking for the objects, but I like the ones with a good story line, where you can lose yourself in it. Some you play as a Princess and you have to save your kingdom from some great evil. Others you have to save the world, or rescue your husband, sister or someone else. There are all sorts of other story lines as well.

I did play a couple on my three and a half inch screen and enjoyed them, but I found the screen a little too small. So two years ago I bought my first tablet, just under eight inch's. I did go down to my local electronics shop and look and try them all out before deciding which one was best for me. Originally, I thought that a seven inch one would be big enough for surfing the internet and playing games on, but from looking at the tablets I realised that seven inches would be too small to surf the internet for me, so I opted for the just under eight inch one. It was the same make as my three and a half inch one, so I was able to download some of my software onto my new devise and have a bigger screen as well, which is much easier to see what you are doing.

To date now I have played around seventy of these type of games. I suppose I like to escape from my life and pretend to be someone else for a short while. In the support group that I go to, there were at one point, about four of the group playing these type of games.

Earlier on in my book, I talked about enjoying reading, I think the reason that I get enjoyment out of reading is escaping into another world again, just like I do in the hidden object games. The real world while you are reading doesn't exist, it's the world in my e-reader that occupies me.

I'm sounding from these two hobbies a bit of a dreamer, which I supposed I am a little bit. I do find myself daydreaming about being someone else, who sells lots of paintings and makes hundreds of thousands pounds and doesn't have to worry about what the future might hold. I suppose we all dream about being someone else, it's probably human nature to do so.

Which brings me onto my painting, which I do every Monday morning and every 2nd and 4th Wednesday evening, at another location in town. My friend Helen comes and picks me up for that one. I seem to find it easier to get on with the people in the two art groups I go to, than I do within the church. In the art groups they mainly just want to talk to you about your painting and not anything personal. In church sometimes they want to know more about you. I then find it difficult to think of things to say. I don't work, people at church must wonder why, as I don't talk about having Asperger's, as I don't think people would understand and some might just think that I was just stupid. I still feel it is greatly misunderstood. In the art groups they don't seem to wonder why I don't work. Most of them are friendly. Helen and two others who go to the Monday group know that I have Asperger's.

I do enjoy going away on holiday. When I'm away I like to do a lot of sightseeing. The last two holidays were in Liverpool and Bristol. I like somewhere with a historical theme or interesting country side. Dad and I have been to Wales and the Lake

Distract. In Wales we stayed in three different places and did over nine hundred miles in my car. We shared the driving, as I'm not a long distance driver, about one and a half hours at a time is enough for me.

I do like to go clothes shopping when I have some money. About three or four times a year, I have a day away from the town, where I live and spend it shopping. Now that I drive, I take the car there, it is within an hour's drive away. Before I used to go by bus which took over an hour to get there and the bus always seemed to take longer to get back home. I supposed more people most have got on the bus going home than they did going. Its better going by car as you can leave home when you want and come back when you want. Plus you don't have to put up with anyone sitting next to you or someone annoying you either. It does cost more going by car, as you have to pay for the car pack. I'm just not a fan of the buses. That's why before I pass my test, I cycled everywhere and it saved on the bus fares as well. Where I live, I heard that it costs now £2.20 one way to go into the town, so it's £4.40 return. It is cheaper to go by car and park for two hours in the car park, for two pounds and I can go when I want.

I have to admit that I do like having gadgets. The minster at church, I think he thinks I'm a gadget girl. A year on he is still talking about my computer, he thinks that I spent way too much on it. He's still I think getting over the shook at how much it cost me. But I wanted to make sure that it lasted and I could still do everything that I wanted on it for as long as possible. My last two computers I had for six and eight years. I paid less for the third one, than I did for the first two. This time I wanted a white lap top computer without a cap between the monitor and keyboard. The minster thought that I wouldn't notice the colour of the computer once I turned it on, I disagree, and I think that I would notice. The other two computers that I had have been desk top computers. This time I wanted one that was portable and I could move it around and use it in my bedroom.

Chapter 46

Final Conclusions and Thoughts

I hope that the children who are born today with Asperger's, have the same chances as everyone else has with jobs and education that I haven't had. Hopefully by the time this generation has grown up, the understanding of the condition will have improved. At the moment most people you meet, sadly don't have a clue and they don't want to know. They just want you to fit in with them, as I look just like everyone else. But I can't fit in just like everyone else, I don't know how. I appear to most people to be able to fit in, but on the inside I'm struggling. It is not something that I can learn to do. I know that most people when they are growing up, learn what to say and when to say it all at the right times. It's not that I'm silly, I just get this mental block when it comes to social situations. I'm better on a one to one, than with a group of people. It's like having a jigsaw puzzle and not being able to put it together, the right way. When everyone else is able to complete the jigsaw and see the picture, I will never be able to see the picture, only a little part. It's not pleasant being on the outside, looking in on the rest of the world and not being able to take part in what others are doing. If I try to go along to social groups, most of the time I feel more isolated, than if I just stay at home. I don't want to stay away, but it's the better of the two evils for me.

I hope this book will help others who have Asperger's, or are waiting to be diagnosed. Also friends, parents, carers and teachers and anyone who comes into contact with someone with Asperger's. Hopefully my life story has given you a better understanding, about how life can be like for others living with Asperger's. Of course it will be different for other people, just like you are an individual so is the person with Asperger's.

Printed in Great Britain
by Amazon.co.uk, Ltd.,
Marston Gate.